To May Davidson

Greetings from the States!

John David Myles

THE TULEYRIES

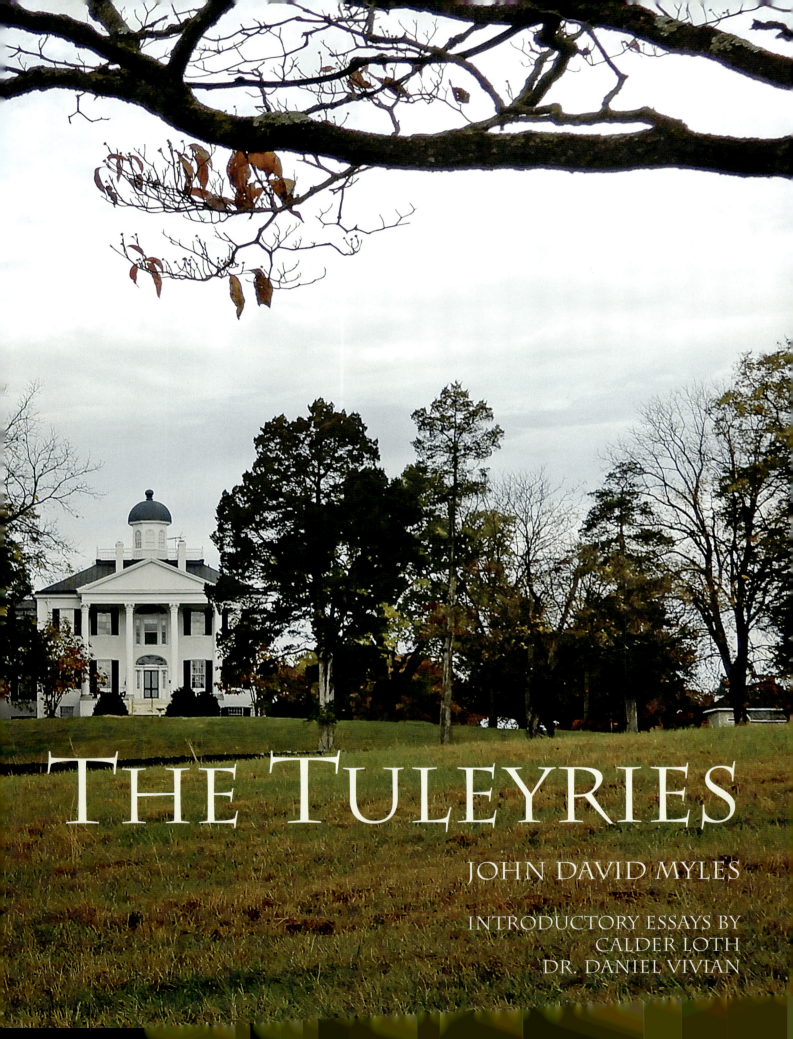

THE TULEYRIES

JOHN DAVID MYLES

INTRODUCTORY ESSAYS BY
CALDER LOTH
DR. DANIEL VIVIAN

ISBN# 978-1-61850-185-1

Library of Congress Control Number: 2021908419

Copy Editor: David A. Bell

Printed in South Korea through
Tailored Group
Louisville, Kentucky

Wild Holly Studio
1908 Webb Road
Simpsonville, Kentucky 40067
jdm@johndavidmyles.com

Table of Contents

East entrance road to The Tuleyries from the Porter Lodge

INTRODUCTION

All houses have histories, and those of houses as large and as ornate as The Tuleyries are generally anything but mundane. The people, enterprises, and events associated with such houses also tend to be thoroughly captivating for a host of reasons. John David Myles's recounting of The Tuleyries's history illustrates these themes well. His narrative weaves together the story of a grand mansion, the families who owned it, and the events that shaped their lives in an insightful, entertaining chronicle of a distinctively American place. Readers will find plenty of interest in the pages that follow.

If there is a lesson to be learned from Myles's work, it lies in the layers of history he has brought to light and the interwoven stories that bind them together. Historians of landscape often speak of the way the past assumes a physical presence in place. Activities spread across time and space leave their imprint, human actions shape spaces of labor and habitation, and time leaves markings of its own. The Tuleyries shows this process clearly. For reasons that seem to owe as much to happenstance and fate as design, many of the buildings and much of the landscape created between Joseph Tuley Sr.'s final years in the 1820s and the Civil War remains intact. At the same time, later owners and others added to the main house, the grounds and outbuildings, and the landscape beyond, each placing his or her stamp on a place where stasis and change comingled, continually vying for the upper hand in a struggle that never reached a clear point of resolution. The result is the complex tapestry that exists today, a record of two centuries of American history and a mélange of commercial, educational, and domestic uses.

Myles's portrait of The Tuleyries is notable for its keen attention to the architecture of the main house and outbuildings, the major figures associated with the property, and events that shaped the form and development of the estate. His investigation of architectural influences, comparisons between the main house and other buildings nearby, and recounting of the saga that befell Mary Tuley as a result of her husband's death and the Civil War make for engrossing reading. The arrival of the Boyces on the scene and the subsequent arrival of Graham and Georgette Blandy connect the Tuleyries to central themes in the history of Gilded Age America. The era inaugurated by Georgette's marriage to Edmund Llewellyn

Bull in 1930 marks yet another transition that immersed The Tuleyries in a sophisticated world of upper-class recreation, elite social connections, and international affairs. Myles touches upon all of these subjects without burdening the narrative nor drawing readers' attention away from The Tuleyries for long. Yet as much as his history deserves praise for its pacing and economy, it also suggests a number of questions that merit further study. Recognizing this is not to detract from Myles's accomplishment but, rather, to suggest how much more The Tuleyries may yet have to offer.

Perhaps the most intriguing question from the era of The Tuleyries's origins concerns Joseph Tuley Sr.'s various enterprises. Tuley's tanneries seems to have been unusually successful, a point suggested by the valuations that Myles mentions from the 1825 inventory of Tuley Sr.'s estate. Presumably, Tuley Sr. also farmed some of his considerable landholdings, and he may also have engaged in land speculation. Whatever the case, it would be useful to know how Tuley amassed property valued at $30,000 at the time of his death. It is possible that the tanneries accounted for most or all of that figure, but it is just as likely that it resulted from a combination of agriculture and industry. A better understanding of Tuley's economic interests would provide valuable context.

A related question concerns the confidence Joseph Tuley Jr. expressed in deciding to build such a large and elegant house for himself and his family. Clearly, the younger Tuley considered himself financially secure, had few apprehensions about the future, and saw himself at the top of the social hierarchy of the northern Shenandoah Valley. The 1845 account from the *Richmond Enquirer* that Myles quotes at length provides a detailed portrait of Tuley's estate and his extensive agricultural interests, offering insight into at least some of the enterprises that supported the handsome residence and the lifestyle he and his family enjoyed. Presumably, much of the planting the *Enquirer* described had been taking place in one form or another since Tuley had inherited the land from his father, and it seems that he also continued operating the tanneries. Still, the degree of refinement Tuley pursued in virtually all aspects of his life and the outlook he must have had in the early 1830s prompts curiosity about the sources of his wealth and social standing. Further inquiry into these subjects might well add to an already intriguing story.

Later developments raise other questions. For students of architecture and anyone attentive to an unexpected oddity, the stepped gables found on several of the outbuildings demand closer study. None are rendered in a manner that suggests a clear connection to the Netherlands, the "Dutch Colonial" strain of the Colonial Revival, or any kind of purposeful symbolism, and yet their styling and execution quickly dispels the temptation to consider them a vernacular innovation that somehow got repeated and developed through successive building campaigns. The fact that they apparently date to 1905 makes them even more curious, particularly in light of the fact that the nearby Wickliffe Church – a possible source of inspiration, as Myles notes – dates to 1846. Put simply, the origin of these features and the campaigns that created the outbuildings that exist today merit sustained investigation. Despite the efforts that John Milner and Associates, Myles, and others have made to try to understand them, it is hard to imagine there is not more to the story than is yet known. Here lies a worthy project for an enterprising graduate student or a devoted researcher in search of a good challenge.

In sum, The Tuleyries is like so many other properties of its kind – a touchstone of memory and history that has more to offer than appearances alone might suggest. The admirable work Myles has done in tracing its origins and development casts light on a saga previously known only to a few and understood well by none. His narrative focuses attention on the major events, people, and themes responsible for the estate that exists today. Yet it is also clear that a more extensive and intricate constellation of histories remains to be discovered. As readers enjoy the story told herein, perhaps some will recognize that further rewards lie waiting, ripe for whomever takes up the challenge of unearthing and sharing them. In the meantime, Myles has crafted an engrossing and edifying history of a truly remarkable estate, an equally remarkable set of families, and a host of other historical actors and events. Reading it is a handsome reward in its own right – and testimony to what Myles has accomplished.

Dr. Daniel J. Vivian
Chair of Historic Preservation
University of Kentucky College of Design

Rear parlor of The Tuleyries in the early 20th century

Christmas at The Tuleyries, 2018

REFLECTIONS
ON A SINGULAR HISTORIC PROPERTY

It is a special compliment to be asked to offer some remarks about The Tuleyries, a singular historic property that I have known for many years. My first encounter with The Tuleyries occurred around 1962 while I was an undergraduate in the University of Virginia's architectural history program. One day my classmate, Peter Hodson, mentioned that he had come across a write-up about a striking northern Virginia mansion called The Tuleyries. The name didn't sound right. I assumed it must be a misspelling of the French royal palace, *The Tuileries*. No, declared Peter, it was built by a man named Tuley. Tuley intended his house to be so impressive that he purposely gave it a catchy name—a double entendre alluding both to a famous palace and his own surname. With my curiosity nudged, I sought more information. John Wayland's well-documented and well-illustrated *Historic Homes of Northern Virginia* (1937), filled me in. I learned that the builder, Joseph Tuley Jr., inherited a lucrative tanning business and sought to display his wealth by creating one of the most imposing residences in the region.

We now fast-forward to 1970 when I was a fledgling architectural historian employed by the Virginia Department of Historic Resources—the commonwealth's official historic preservation office. In June of that year, the estate's owner, Mrs. Orme Wilson Sr., contacted James Moody, the department's director, expressing her concern that the Virginia Department of Highways intended to condemn the estate's frontage along U.S. Route 50 for two additional highway lanes. She was distressed that the project would remove much of The Tuleyries' forested buffer stretched along the highway. I felt smart telling Mr. Moody that I knew about The Tuleyries and its odd name. Moody soon visited Mrs. Wilson and advised her that a less invasive solution might be negotiated if Mrs. Wilson considered donating a preservation easement on the property. The easement could offer legal protection against such encroachment. I was subsequently tasked to work with Mrs. Wilson on the matter. The assignment resulted in my first visit to the place.

To say that I was impressed both by The Tuleyries and Mrs. Wilson would be an understatement. The house and its chatelaine were both captivating. It was a scene from a bygone era. Little had changed at The Tuleyries either in lifestyle or setting since the beginning of the century. We duly discussed the easement program during which I couldn't resist ogling the array of surrounding architectural details. Mrs. Wilson offered that she would consider the easement. In the meantime, my department proceeded to initiate official landmark designation for the estate. The Tuleyries was thus added to the Virginia Landmarks Register in 1971 and the National Register of Historic Places in 1972. Because these designations were primarily honorific, they would not automatically stop the highway project but we hoped they could influence it. Nevertheless, no action was taken on an easement donation and the highway design progressed. After several years, the extra lanes were finally constructed. Fortunately, the encroachment was kept to a minimum, preserving enough of the forest depth to maintain an acceptable visual buffer.

Working on the landmark designations provided me an opportunity to ponder what made The Tuleyries exceptional. What significance did it have to the state and nation to warrant such official recognition? It was curious that a house so imposing and sophisticated had no prominent architect involved with its design. What became obvious, and noteworthy, was that its owner, Joseph Tuley Jr., was architecturally literate and succeeded much on his own in creating a setting that suitably signaled his success. His use of a monumental Corinthian portico and domed cupola declared that this was the home of a person of prominence. The mansion's various interior features—its domed entrance hall, the spiral stair, the plasterwork cornices, the ceiling decorations, and the unusual oval colonnettes flanking the parlor windows coalesced into a visually engaging architectural sequence. Moreover, the estate's historic ancillary structures formed a rare surviving plantation complex.

As for its historic significance, it can't be claimed that The Tuleyries was the scene of great historic events. The only Civil War action it witnessed was Union soldiers burning its fields. Instead, the estate derived its distinction from being a social document of an elite way of life spanning nearly two centuries. Its various owners and their families enjoyed the activities and trappings of a gentry lifestyle that is still evident in the estate's many physical components. Adding to its layers was the Tuleyries' bucolic setting—intact and well maintained.

My next encounter with The Tuleyries came soon after Mrs. Wilson died in 1987, having lived a century. Her son, Orme Wilson Jr. who inherited the property, invited me to consult on his plans to make The Tuleyries his primary residence. The elder Mrs. Wilson had used the house mainly as a summer retreat; few changes or upgrades had been made over the years. The goal was to correct various structural issues, modernize the systems, and undertake the conservation of historic architectural fabric. I made a thorough inspection of the house with Mr. Wilson and sent him contact information for several architectural firms specializing in historic restoration. Of these, Wilson chose John Milner Associates, a happy choice. Milner and his team undertook a textbook restoration, completing it early in 1991. Just two months later, with shock and regret, I learned that Mr. Wilson had died suddenly, just days before he and his wife planned to move into their new home.

I was able to visit the mansion again in July of 1991 to see the restoration. Orme Wilson's widow ("Midge") was unable to be there to show me around but arranged to have someone take me through. I later wrote her that halfway through the visit I had run out of superlatives. I said that I had dealt with many restoration projects but The Tuleyries ranks with the finest, especially considering that some seventy-five percent of the work was invisible. This included the extensive structural repairs guaranteeing that the house will last another century or more. The interior treatments and appointments reflected an insouciant patrician taste so right for the place.

The Tuleyries is now entering the next phase of its history. We trust the house will welcome its new owners and that they will love the place as much as have many predecessors.

Calder Loth
Senior Architectural Historian, retired
Virginia Department of Historic Resources

Eastern facade of The Tuleyries, *courtesy of John Milner Architects*

PROLOGUE

More than a century and three quarters after it was built on a rise facing the Blue Ridge in what soon thereafter became Clarke County, Virginia, The Tuleyries still accomplishes what must have been Colonel Tuley's original intention. It casts a benign but imposing glance across the valley which provided the wealth which made it possible. It immediately informs the viewer that the builder either was familiar with the rules of architecture and prevailing fashion or knew he had to find someone who was to help him complete his vision. Above all, it tells all who pass by that Col. Joseph Tuley, son of a tanner and a tanner himself, had reached the level of wealth and prominence of his more established neighbors, the Burwells, Carters, and other descendants of Virginia's first families who were already long established in this beautiful country. Colonel Tuley had either the misfortune of dying in 1860 at the relatively young age of 64 or the good timing to leave the beautiful world he had created shortly before it came crashing down around him.

Colonel Tuley having no children of his own, his plantation ultimately passed to the family of a niece who in many ways exemplified the era of rebuilding and improvement after the Civil War. After the century turned, a New York broker and his young wife set about recreating and expanding the Colonel's dream. There were orchards and cattle and gardens and all manner of entertainments. The house was brought up to date with a shocking three bathrooms on the second floor. The broker left the house and immediately surrounding land to his wife, at whose death they passed to her sister. For the third quarter of the 20th century, The Tuleyries was a wasp in amber, preserved and unchanging. In the late 1980s, the next generation completed a remarkable restoration of the house. After another untimely death in 1991, The Tuleyries slipped back into amber. Today, another generation is again lavishing attention on the house and estate.

Through it all, Colonel Tuley's house has survived and welcomed countless visitors who have been taken by its beauty. The stories of its inhabitants are entwined with the stories of its construction and evolution. This chronicle hopes to tell these stories casting light on the survival of one of Virginia's architectural treasures as it prepares to enter its third century in the valley.

THE TULEYS

The first Tuleys to reach America were three brothers fleeing France, likely after the revocation of the Edict of Nantes. They are said to have landed in South Carolina and, from there, one went to Louisiana, one went to New York, and one named Peter went to Virginia. By 1729, a Thomas Tuley was living in New Jersey but family chronicler, William Floyd Tuley in his 1906 *The Tuley Family Memoirs,* was unable to determine whether he descended from the brother who went to New York or the brother who settled in Virginia. Regardless, Thomas had a son, Jonathan, who had a son, Joseph. With him, the story of The Tuleyries begins.

The few details known of this Joseph, later known as Joseph Tuley Sr., were gleaned in the mid-1930s from court documents and land records by R. E. Griffith Sr. who did extensive research on The Tuleyries lands at the request of a later owner. Griffith summed up the senior Tuley's advent in Clarke County by saying that, "It would appear that he arrived in Virginia with a small inheritance, little education and a tremendous capacity for making money." Born in Burlington County, New Jersey, in 1763, Tuley was known by 1786 in what was then Frederick County as a tanner. From the time of his arrival, he associated with Col. Nathaniel Burwell, owner of Carter Hall and General Daniel Morgan of Saratoga. Burwell was the great-grandson of Robert "King" Carter of Corotoman who served as agent for the Northern Neck Proprietary for Lord Fairfax. Morgan was revered as the hero of the battles of Saratoga and Cowpens during the Revolutionary War.

On Christmas Day, 1787, Joseph Sr. married Ann Brownley or Brownlee. He and Ann had eleven children of whom five survived to adulthood. Their only surviving son, Joseph Jr., and daughter, Sarah Goen Tuley Wright, later played crucial roles in the history of The Tuleyries. It is unknown where Joseph and Ann, also known as Nancy, first lived. In 1786, he had two acres of land adjacent to the Burwell-Morgan mill on Spout Run in Millwood surveyed. In 1789, he leased those two acres from Col. Burwell along with a "plentiful supply of water from the mill race for a tanyard." It is again unclear whether Col. Burwell already had a tanyard on the site or whether Joseph established it upon taking possession of the property. Tuley had the site surveyed again and in 1793 when he leased slightly more than four acres from Col.

"Three Pounds", the home of Joseph Tuley Sr., Millwood, Virginia

Burwell for three pounds per year. This property included the site across the creek upon which he built a house overlooking the tanyard and the mill. Subsequent owners have used the consideration for this lease as the name of the house. Its exact date is also unknown but tradition holds that Joseph Tuley Jr. was born in the house in 1796.

The purchases in Millwood were just the beginning for Mr. Tuley. In 1795, he acquired 757 acres of land in the nearby village of Paris and bought another 477 acres in what is now Hampshire County, West Virginia, in 1799. He purchased the first lands associated with The Tuleyries in 1806. It appears that his wife's inheritance from her father, John Brownley, enabled him to purchase 411 acres from Alexander Henderson described as part of the Rattle Snake Springs tract. This was the beginning of The Tuleyries.

In 1810, Tuley Sr. purchased an additional 211-acre portion of the Rattle Snake Springs tract which came to be known as Tanner's Retreat. He acquired the tract by paying the debts of one Major Henry Bartlett, then in debtors' prison. Griffith suggests that Tuley moved into Bartlett's dwelling at Tanner's Retreat and Stuart E. Brown Jr. states in *Annals of Clarke County, Vol. 1*, that he expanded the residence. The location of Bartlett's home and later fate are unknown. Even if Tuley did move his family to the Rattle Snake Springs tract, he did not sell his home in Millwood, which remained in the family until after the Civil War. He also acquired large tracts of land in Kentucky and another 500-acre farm in Augusta County. Along the way, he apparently tried his hand at inventing, having received a patent in 1814 for a "family stove" - whatever that may have been. In 1819, he purchased land in Front Royal on which a tannery may have already been in existence.

Altogether, when he died in June of 1825, he was able to leave his wife, son, and three of his four daughters considerable property each. His will, dated February 26, 1823, and probated October 31, 1825, left his wife a 211-acre tract "by the name of the Grove" along with two families of negro slaves and various livestock and half of the household and kitchen goods as she should choose. Daughter Mary Mitchell received land in Staunton and her sons received land on the Licking River in Kentucky. Daughter Belinda Strother's sons also received Kentucky lands on the Green River. Daughter Sarah Wright received the tanyard property in Front Royal and land in Hampshire County. Each of the daughters also received 35 shares in the Ashby's Gap turnpike. The residue of Tuley's property, including the 211 acres left to Nancy for life, went to his son, Joseph Jr. Evidencing the continued connection between the Tuleys and the Burwells, Joseph Sr. named his "good friend" Nathaniel Burwell, son of the Nathaniel who first leased him land in Millwood, as his executor. No one today knows why daughter Louzetta Massie was not mentioned in the will.

Whether there were two 211-acre tracts soon became a moot point as Ann "Nancy" Tuley followed her husband to the graveyard at the Old Chapel Cemetery near Millwood in October of 1825 and the Grove passed to Joseph Jr. In addition to his lands, Joseph Sr. left a considerable estate of personal property. The scope of his tanning operations is indicated by the 1,000 cords of black and chestnut oak bark valued at $3,500 in his inventory. He also died possessed of more than forty slaves and various of their children. The total value of his inventory as appraised in December 1825 was $30,418.25.

As little is known of the early life of Joseph Tuley Jr. as is known about his father's. One can surmise that he remained closely associated with the Burwell family and, given his own success in the business, he evidently learned the tanning trade well. An unsigned typescript in the files at The Tuleyries dated 1936 and likely by Griffith, states that in 1826, the then thirty-year-old Tuley was promoted from major to lieutenant colonel in the 122nd Regiment of the Virginia Militia, suggesting that he was highly esteemed by his neighbors and had been part of the militia for some time prior. He seems to have taken the honor seriously as he was referred to as Col. Tuley for the rest of his days.

The Colonel's scope of activity must have been considerably broader than just tanning and Clarke County. His stepdaughter wrote years later that he had purchased a Gilbert Stuart portrait of George Washington at a New York auction in 1825. Tradition holds that around 1830, he married Mary Wheeler Edelen (Edelin) Jackson, widow of Dr. John S. Jackson, an army surgeon. As it turns out, the name is right but the date is wrong. John S. Jackson of North Carolina received a Doctor of Medicine degree from the University of Pennsylvania in 1821 and married Mary Edelin on May 4, 1824, in the District of Columbia. Dr. Jackson served as a surgeon's mate in the 4th Infantry, U. S. Army, following his graduation and later became an assistant surgeon. He died in 1832 and is buried in the Montgomery Cemetery in Oakland City, Indiana.

During 1832, the 4th Infantry was stationed in New Orleans and became involved in the Black Hawk War when two of its divisions were sent to Fort Crawford in Prairie du Chien, Wisconsin. After service there, the troops returned to Rock Island, Illinois, where there was a cholera outbreak. Whether Jackson remained in New Orleans or went with the two divisions sent north and how and why he ended up in southwestern Indiana and what happened to him there are all mysteries. However, we do know that he and Mary had three children, Mary Tuley Jackson (1825-1905), Westel Willoughby Jackson (1826-1866), and J.

Joseph Tuley Jr. by Jane Stuart, *courtesy of the Clarke County Historical Association Portrait Collection*

Mary Wheeler Edelin Jackson Tuley by Charles Bird King, *courtesy of Mrs. F. W. McM. Woodrow*

Edwards Jackson (1828-1856). None of them married and all were buried in the Tuley plot at the Old Chapel Cemetery.

Mary's tombstone at Old Chapel states that she was born in 1810. If one is to believe what is carved in stone, she must have married at the tender age of 14 or 15 and have had three children and lost a husband by the time she was 22. A native of St. Mary's City, Maryland's first capital, Mary and her family were likely living in Washington, D.C., when Jackson died. A widow in her early twenties with three small children, her circumstances must have been such that a marriage proposal from a wealthy militia colonel and farmer from Clarke County, even one fourteen years her senior and a tanner by trade and heritage, was very appealing. The prospect of living at the Colonel's newly built house must also have been tempting. She and the Colonel were married on April 20, 1835, in Washington.

It is tempting to think that the lovely portrait of Mary Tuley was painted to celebrate the wedding. It was once attributed to Thomas Sully but is now said to be the work of Charles Bird King, a Rhode Islander who settled in Washington, D. C., in 1818 after studying with Benjamin West in London. Along the way, he painted the portraits of a virtual who's who of Washington's political and social worlds. Sitters included President Monroe, Dolley Madison, President and Mrs. John Quincy Adams, Daniel Webster, Henry Clay, John C. Calhoun, and the Marquis de Lafayette, as well as Carters, Tayloes, and the first Nathaniel Burwell of Carter Hall. He is perhaps best remembered today for approximately 100 portraits of Native Americans who visited Washington, many of which were reproduced as lithographs in the *History of the Indian Tribes of North America* published between 1836 and 1844.

The Colonel's portrait is attributed to Jane Stuart, daughter of the esteemed Gilbert Stuart. Jane was considered the most talented of Stuart's children. Although best known for copies of her father's portraits of George and Martha Washington, she also painted numerous other portraits. She lived and worked in Boston and Newport, Rhode Island, and when and where the Colonel sat for her are unknown. Both of these portraits remained in the families of collateral descendants of Colonel Tuley until the mid-1940s and Mary's continues to be cherished by the family. The current whereabouts of the Colonel's are unknown. Stylistically, the Stuart portrait appears to be of an earlier date and may have been painted on the trip to the Northeast in 1825 when Tuley is said to have purchased a Stuart portrait of George Washington by Jane Stuart's father. The painting of Mary, in which she holds an ivory fan, wears a brilliant pink gown, and has a garland of flowers in her hair, is a much looser composition intended to capture her beauty and charm.

Regardless of when the portraits were painted, preparations for constructing the new house on the Rattle Snake Springs tract were well underway in 1832. Two of Joseph Tuley's account books survive at The Tuleyries. A card stored with the later one reads, "Gave me Tuley acct book Brown Morton, III Waterford Va -." Morton, an internationally known preservation consultant and former professor at the University of Mary Washington in Fredericksburg, Virginia, came across the ledger at an antique shop near Charlottesville in the mid-1960s and later passed it along to Mrs. Orme Wilson Sr. The fascinating book led to a long friendship between the two.

This ledger has entries from the late 1820s into the 1850s. It was succeeded by Tuley's "Red Back" ledger sometime in the late 1840s. The whereabouts of that book are unknown. Tuley kept meticulous if sometimes inscrutable accounts in often illegible handwriting. He traded with virtually all of the people in the neighborhood - Burwells, Pages, Trenarys, Kerfoots, Sowers, etc. There are endless entries which appear to show Tuley selling finished leathers, often for harness and

Colonel Tuley's ledger with references to construction tabbed

TULEYRIES ACCOUNT BOOK ENTRIES
(Identifiable as relating to the construction of the main house)

1832	William Broy - 12,000 feet ¼, 1, 1 ½, and 2 inch pine and poplar boards and scantling - $190.00
7/4/1832	Dan'l P. Conrad - nails - $26.25 ½
8/13/1832	Adam Steel - 3500 lathes - $7.00
10/1832	J. B. T. Reed - copper globe, putting on 45 squares plus 69 feet of tin roof, brazing and soldering 566 lbs of copper, etc. - $272.25
10/10/1832	Harrison Anderson - 5,000 shingles - $15.00
1833	Symington & Taylor - marble flagging for portico 37 feet long by 17 feet wide $310.00, 4 whole & 2 half bases - $130.00, 4 whole & 2 half plinths - $70.00, 1 large door sill - $25.00, 1 large Venetian window sill - $9.00, cornice around portico - $150.00, shipping and blocking - $361.60 = $1,055.60
6/15/1833	John Kerfoot - 15 bushels plaster - $18.75
6/29/1833	Adam Steel - 3000 lathes - $6.00
7/20/1833	John Kerfoot - 5 ½ bushels plaster $6.87½
9/1833	Peter Royston - hauling 10 boxes of marble - $7.00 per ton - $30.95- hauling 250 "la" white lead - $1.00
10/2/1833	Jno. Fletcher - painting my building complete - $450.00
10/2/1833	Isaac Kurts - turning blocks for building - $36.37
10/24/1833	John W. Cockerell - 391,004 brick in building - $3,323.89, 52,872 brick in stable = $396.54
1/27/1834	William Morrison - lot mahogany $90.00
2/20/1834	William Trenary - building smoke house and two wings, flue in smoke house, and work under portico - $33.33
7/1/1834	Symington & Taylor - 2 stone cutters (?) steps and flagging 25 days - $100.00, 2 Egyptian + 2 Phila. mantels with soap stone and hearths complete - $577.50, 2 black column shelves unfortunately broken - $25.00, 18 days charge for putting up mantels - $36.00
7/20/1834	John Gill - bill for plastering and stucco work - $911.00
8/14/1834	Bill from James Trenary dressing for stone - $2.00
9/28/1834	John W. Cockerell - an extra account of turning arches & brick - $20.00
9/30/1834	carriage - 4,306 lbs marble - $19.90
11/27/1834	Symington & Taylor - freight, labour, storage & portage - $19.28
4/2/1835	H. L. Wyatt - 6,700 short shingles - $23.00
4/28/1835	H. L. Wyatt - 10,000 short shingles - $35.00
6/15/1835	Wm. Trenary - lay marble Portico - $5.00
11/20/1835	G. Drake - 162 yds rough cast - $20.14, 71 yds plastering - $7.10, 100 yds rough - $3.00, repairs in dwelling - $2.00 = $32.24
11/21/1836	Samuel Yeagle - soldering copper gutters on the house - $1.50

shoes, in return for skins of every kind, including dog, and bark used in the tannery. There are also seemingly endless loads of wood which he both bought and sold, as well as grain, flour, and bacon.

Hidden away within these transactions are a number which appear to relate to the construction of The Tuleyries and subsequent additions to it but they are sometimes contradictory and establish the date on which accounts were paid, rather than when work was done or materials supplied. The first identifiable entry is for 12,000 feet of lumber sometime in 1832. In October of that year, Col. Tuley paid J. B. T. Reed for a copper globe and putting on 45 squares and 69 feet of tin roof. On the other hand, a 1965 letter from Truxton Boyce quotes a *Winchester Virginian* clipping dated March 5, 1834, in which, "Geo. and Tilden Reed say they have just covered the new dwelling house of Col. Joseph Tuley with Tin." The globe at least related to the cupola atop the house and would indicate that at least the structure was complete by 1832. Suffice it to say, it would have been unusual for the cupola to be completed before the rest of the roof. Tuley did not pay John W. Cockerell for "brick in building" and "brick in stable" until October 1834. Regardless, the construction appears to have been underway by the summer of 1832 and essentially completed by the end of 1834. It is interesting to note that the charge from Symington & Taylor of Baltimore for the pair of black marble mantels in the double parlor and two others was the most expensive individual entry noted in the ledger excepting only the payment for brick.

One of the pair of Greek Revival mantels purchased from Symington & Taylor for the double parlor at The Tuleyries and described as "Egyptian" in Col. Tuley's ledger

Into what sort of house were these mantels installed and who designed it? As to the latter question, there is the slight possibility that David Meade, brother of William Meade, Bishop of Virginia, may have had a hand in the process. He is credited with designing the Clarke County Courthouse between the creation of Clarke County from Frederick County in 1836 and his death in 1837. The design of the courthouse shows considerable familiarity with the proper use of the Tuscan order and the building has doors with the same arrangement of panels as those at The Tuleyries. There are similar doors at nearby Greenway Court dating to 1828 and at Clifton, a house contemporaneous with The Tuleyries. Perhaps the best answer to the question is nobody knows.

We have a fairly good idea of the house into which the Tuleys moved. Samuel Kercheval,

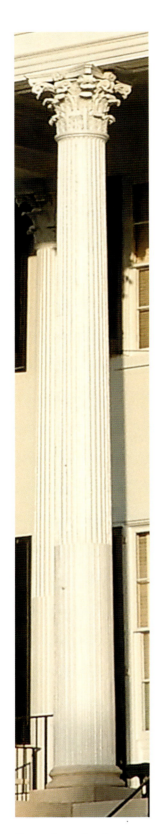

Stop-fluted column
at The Tuleyries

in the second edition of his 1850 *History of the Valley*, described the house as "... a most splendid and expensive mansion on his beautiful farm in the neighborhood of Millwood, which he has named the 'Tuleyries.' ... [T]his edifice is sixty feet by forty, of the best brick - finished from the base to the attic in the most elegant style of modern architecture, and is covered with tin." At 60 feet x 40 feet, a measurement likely carried over from Kercheval's first edition, the original house consisted of the two rooms on either side of the central hall which ran the depth of the house. The English basement, which was fully lit, contained the kitchen and various service rooms. The first floor, reached up white marble steps rising to a marble-floored porch, consisted of the same four rooms and hall as did the second floor. From the rear of the first-floor hall, a spiral staircase rises to the third or attic floor where a separate stair gives access to the octagonal cupola which crowns the hip roof.

The elegance and sometime paradoxically awkward proportions of The Tuleyries may best be understood by comparing it with another elegant house, Clifton, which was built at the same time in the same county and bears a close resemblance, down to the fact that the doors at the rear of the first-floor halls are slightly off center to accommodate the staircases. Both are distinguished by tetrastyle porticoes. However, these could hardly be more different. The Tuscan portico at Clifton is much heavier while at the same time its entablature is too shallow for the pediment it supports. The Tuleyries, on the other hand, has a well-developed entablature but its fluted Corinthian columns are considerably narrower than classical rules would require.

The most interesting feature of the columns at The Tuleyries is the cabling or stop- or double-fluting which runs from their stone bases one-third of the way up their shafts. This is an extremely rare feature in American architecture before the influence of the *Ecole des Beaux Arts* became dominant toward the end of the 19th century although it was used with some frequency by 18th-century cabinetmakers. Its most famous early use is in the interior of Rome's Pantheon as rebuilt by the Emperor Hadrian circa 120 A.D. Raphael was so taken with the building that he chose to be buried there and it was the inspiration for his Chigi Chapel at Santa Maria del Popolo where the pilasters feature stop-fluting.

Sir Christopher Wren used cabling on the columns at the entry and the interior pilasters at St. Paul's Cathedral begun in 1675. However, it appears only once in *Vitruvius Britannicus* on the facade of the Powis House in London built the year before Colen Campbell published the first volume of his great work in 1715. By mid-century, cabling was discussed in leading English architectural works. Isaac Ware, in *A Complete Body of Architecture* published in 1756, defined

Detail from *The Choir of St. Paul's Cathedral. Le Choeur de la Cathedrale de St. Paul a Londre.* (Carrington Bowles, engraver, London, 1754) showing stop-fluting on interior pilasters

cabling as "The filling up the middle of a fluting in a column with something like a rope, hence a column whose flutings are filled up are called columns with cabled flutings." He was apparently not fond of fluting in general and even less so of cabling.

> *There is but one reason that can be alledged in [flutings'] favor, that is, they have an air of lightness: but if the column be proportioned rightly, its own aspect is just as light as it should be. It were an odd humour to make it originally too heavy, in order to scoop away some of its surface to make it lighter.*
>
> *These flutings have the best appearance when they are cabled, that is filled up, at least to a certain height: but if they were to be filled up, to what purpose were they made? They impair the great simplicity of the columns, and they have no foundation in reason: therefore they are a false ornament.*
>
> *This is judging with severity, but it is judging with truth.*

After all that, Ware provided an illustration of cabling which he associated with the Ionic order.

Soon thereafter, in 1759, William Chambers published the first version of his *Treatise on Civil Architecture*. While he associated cabling with the Corinthian order, he was less critical and gave a practical explanation for its use. All in all, he seems not to have been a great fan either. "The Flutings may be filled to one third of their Height with cabling, as in the inside of the Pantheon; which will strengthen the lower part of the Column, and make it less liable to injury. But if the Columns are not within reach or subject to be hurt by passengers, they are better omitted for the general Hue of the column will then be more even."

In Virginia, the first known use of cabling is on interior woodwork at the Thomas Nelson house in Yorktown, dating from 1730. However, Colonel Tuley's columns likely owe their design to those on the portico at Oatlands in nearby Loudoun County. These were added to the house in 1827 by its builder, George Carter. It is not known if Carter had access to Ware's *A Complete Body of Architecture* which had the illustration of cabling but he is said to have relied on Chambers' *Treatise* when he expanded his home at that time. The Oatlands columns, like those at The Tuleyries, are Corinthian but carry a full academic entablature. Their capitals were ordered by Carter from Henry Farnham of Grand Street, New York. In his letter to Farnham, Carter states that the bases for his columns had already been cut but not by whom.

Given the proximity of Oatlands to White Post, the family relationship between George Carter and Tuley's friend Col. Burwell (their great-grandfather was Robert "King" Carter), the similarity between the columns at The Tuleyries and at Oatlands, and finally the rarity of the use of cabling, one can only assume that Tuley was aware of the portico at Oatlands and took the designs for his columns from it. While we know where Carter obtained his capitals, we do not know who carved Tuley's. On the other hand, we don't know who produced Carter's bases but have an entry in Tuley's ledger stating that his were purchased from Symington & Taylor in Baltimore.

Returning to Clifton, both houses have the same footprint but The Tuleyries is much taller, a fact emphasized by the higher pitch of its hip roof which rises to a balustraded viewing platform around the cupola. The hip roof is in fact steeper than the roof of the portico. The roof at Clifton on the other hand has a flatter pitch than its portico pediment. Both houses have interior chimneys but these again produce different results. Those at The Tuleyries are located in the hall walls while those at Clifton are in the walls dividing the rooms on either

Clifton, northeastern Clarke County   The Tuleyries, southwestern Clarke County

side of the hall, leaving those at Clifton to underline the width of the house while those at The Tuleyries lead the eye directly to the cupola. The windows at both houses have six-over-six sash and the windows on either side of their entries have hinged panels which allow direct access to the porches, but the windows at The Tuleyries are considerably larger.

Above all, both literally and figuratively, The Tuleyries is dominated by its remarkable cupola. Virginia had an early tradition of public buildings topped by these architectural ornaments. The famous Bodleian Plate, a 1740 English engraving of buildings at Williamsburg, shows tall cupolas atop the capitol, Governor's Palace, and College of William and Mary. The originals of all three were long gone by the time Col. Tuley set about building but arguably the most famous, public or private, George Washington's at Mount Vernon, still afforded views up and down the Potomac. To indulge in understatement, the mere existence of the cupola at The Tuleyries is remarkable and its survival, against the winds of time and fashion, equally so. Which is not to say that it is necessarily a thing of superb proportions. Its roof seems a cloche a couple of sizes too large for it, an effect not relieved by the copper globe which takes the place of the expected vane.

At neither house does the portico entablature continue around the front and side walls. While the cornices at both houses are approximately the same size, that at Clifton is composed of standard molding profiles ornamented only by a string of beading. The carpenters at The Tuleyries went wild. Rope rests atop a guilloche and another rope surmounts the lowest element, a delicately carved pattern consisting of thousands of small pieces, carved and applied by hand, which also appears at the entry at Oatlands. Between these elements, the carpenters have inserted the deeply cut layered elements which reappear on the mantels of both houses and give them the local name of Winchester or knife-shelf mantels.

Exactly when or why Winchester laid claim to this particular detail is unknown. It is said to evoke the annulets or incised bands at the point where a Greek Doric capital rests upon the column shaft. It was first illustrated in the *Antiquities of Athens* published in London in 1762 and based on measured drawings of ancient monuments in the city made by James Stuart and Nicholas Revett from 1751 to 1753 and republished many

Winchester or knife-shelf mantel at Clifton   Knife-shelf mantel at The Tuleyries

times over the years. The feature was commonly used on mantels during the progression from the Adamsesque colonettes of the Federal period to the later heavier and simpler columns of the Greek Revival.

At Clifton, the carpenters took the mantel form and had a field day at the main entrance, making it the center of attention. The sidelights and elliptical fan are framed by

Doric capital with annulets at the Parthenon in Athens, *courtesy of Calder Loth*

Clifton's exterior cornice

The Tuleyries' exterior cornice

Entry at Clifton

Entry at The Tuleyries

17

freestanding fluted columns and support a reeded architrave spanning the fan. A tripartite window is placed above the entry at the same level as the other second-floor windows.

At The Tuleyries, similar doors, sidelights, and fan are unembellished beyond the opening in the wall. However, the window above the entry at The Tuleyries, also tripartite, rises from floor level and has its own fan, giving yet one more vertical element to the composition. Combined with the much higher second-floor ceilings, it provides a stunning view of the mountains from the upper hall.

The rear facade at Clifton is five bay like the front and features a full Palladian window above the rear entry, making this side of the house at least as appealing as the front. It is impossible without some destructive detective work to reconstruct the original rear facade of The Tuleyries. The placement of doors from the rear of the current dining room and of the northwest bedroom suggests that before additions were made to the rear of the house there were two bays to the right of the rear entry and only one to the left, an arrangement found at another house in Clarke County, Smithfield. Mention of Smithfield brings one to a feature which appears at all three of these Clarke County houses: carved woodwork with columns which are oval in section rather than round.

Second-floor hall at The Tuleyries

Mantel at Smithfield

Hall column at Clifton

Window frame at The Tuleyries

Stair bracket at The Tuleyries

Stair bracket at Clifton

The southwest wall of the front parlor

Smithfield, a house virtually identical to Clifton in plan, was completed in 1824, almost a decade before Clifton and The Tuleyries were constructed. The oval columns there were used on either side of the entry door, supporting an arch which divides the central hall, and on one of the mantels. Similarly, at Clifton, they appear on a mantel and supporting the arch which divides the central hall. At The Tuleyries, their use is limited to the window and door frames in the double parlors, but there the eight window frames and the frames for the massive doors which divide the parlors are nothing short of spectacular. One devoutly wishes that the carver of these columns and their source were known.

While the source of the oval columns has not been identified, the stair brackets at both Clifton and The Tuleyries came directly from Plate 31 of Owen Biddle's *Young Carpenter's Guide*. First published in 1805, a year before Biddle's death, this book and some of its designs have long outlived him. It went through several printings including an 1815 edition published by Johnson & Warner of Richmond which is likely the copy that was floating around the Shenandoah Valley when these houses were built. In 1833, it was expanded by architect John Haviland and republished in Philadelphia. The stair bracket appears as Plate 31 in the original edition and as Plate 42 in the later book. It was copied at Bremo in Fluvanna County as early as 1815. The book and the bracket were also popular in Jefferson County, West Virginia. The builders of Bel-Mar, the Jacob Moler house (1834), and Western View (1831), both incorporated the design in the houses' main stairways. Bel-Mar has knife-shelf mantels virtually identical to those at The Tuleyries as do two other houses near Shepherdstown, the

Southeast wall of the front parlor seen between the doors which can separate the rooms

Dr. John R. Hayden house (1826) and Woodbury (1833). Whether the same carpenters were building in both places at the same time or simply using the same book is unknown although the distance between Shepherdstown and White Post is only around 35 miles. It is clear that the book traveled much farther, the bracket design having been used in a lost home built by grandparents of President Truman in Shelby County, Kentucky prior to 1830. The knife-shelf also made its way across the mountains, used on a mantel in a Louisville townhouse recorded in the Historic American Buildings Survey.

Regardless of the sources of the oval columns, the double parlors at The Tuleyries are in fact spectacular. In the first instance, the windows in the house are unusually large. Locating the chimneys in the hall wall allowed inclusion of two windows per outside wall of each for a total of eight which originally flooded the room with daylight. There are the beautifully carved "Egyptian" mantels on the pair of fireplaces whose Ionic columns complement the woodwork, and finally there are the pair of massive mahogany doors which separate the two rooms when closed. Encircled by plaster cornices with an anthemion and lotus frieze, the parlors were described as "among the state's most historic rooms" in a 1991 letter from Calder Loth, noted authority on historic architecture in Virginia. In the midst of this grandeur and attention to detail, it is puzzling to note that the chimneys are not centered on their walls leaving the mantels, which are, off-center of the projecting chimneys.

The architectural unity of the parlors is broken only by the reeded frames of the doors leading to the central hall. Complete with bull's eye corner blocks, they nonetheless pale by

Mantel in the rear parlor

comparison to the window frames where the Ionic columns support a full entablature with a pulvinated frieze. They are used throughout the original house and are right at home in the other room about which Loth was so enthusiastic, the entry hall. In contrast to the unity achieved in the parlors, this room is divided into two visually distinct sections. Immediately inside the front doors, one sees a very shallow, ribbed dome. The effect is enhanced by the four elliptical arches which rest on an architrave which runs between the fan and the entry doors and continues around the side walls of the hall until it terminates in a pair of wide pilasters which support a coffered arch. The pendentives, now painted a pale blue, emphasize the effect. It is a conceit worthy of Benjamin Henry Latrobe or Sir John Soane which therefore bears no relationship to the magnificent woodwork next door.

Although Latrobe had corresponded in 1811 with Robert Carter Burwell about plans for nearby Long Branch, the architect died in New Orleans in 1820. Soane lived until 1837 but is not known to have had any connection to America, let alone Clarke County, Virginia. The Tuleys could have seen examples of Latrobe's work at the Baltimore Cathedral or the U. S. Capitol or other nearby Virginia and Maryland houses now lost. However, the affinity between the entry at The Tuleyries and that at Decatur House on Jackson Square in the District of Columbia is particularly striking. Whoever drew the plans for this element of The Tuleyries must have been familiar with it but lacked either the training or the discipline of Latrobe. There are various differences between the two: Latrobe carried the door frames into the entablature from which his arches spring and the arch which divides the hall at Decatur House is not coffered. The most striking difference is that Latrobe ended the division between front and rear halls with an apse with niches and curved doors, beyond which the stair rises and behind it, the rear doors are centered. This feature, which reiterates the elements used in the hall, was dispensed with at The Tuleyries, perhaps because the builders were so proud of their spiral staircase.

Decatur House was completed in 1818 but Commodore Stephen Decatur was killed in a duel in 1820. His wife rented the house thereafter and because of its proximity to the White House, it became a very fashionable spot. It is said to have become the unofficial residence of the secretaries of state, having been rented to Henry Clay, Martin Van Buren, and Edward Livingston between 1827 and 1833 while each served in that position. Given the later-documented involvement of the Tuleys in Washington social life, it seems likely they were among the many entertained and may even have met there during this period.

Rather than complete the temple effect of the entry at Decatur House, the dividing arch at The Tuleyries serves to frame the stairway which ascends the right hand wall and spirals within a curved well to the third floor. Quite a stairway it is but one can easily imagine how magnificent it would have been if centered beneath and lit from the cupola atop the house. This, of course, would have required a complete rethinking of the plan of the house. Due to later changes, it is unknown whether further disparate decorative elements were used in what were two rooms to the right of the hall or if the two "Phila. mantels" ordered from Symington and Taylor were used there. However, the window and door frames which appear to be original match the door frames in the parlors and hall and the distinctive doors with their six small panels above a pair of taller ones below are used throughout the second floor's hall and four chambers. While it will never receive any awards for architectural consistency, the various elements incorporated by Col. Tuley and others added in later years give the house a fascinating complexity few other houses can boast.

Entry "dome" at The Tuleyries

Entry at Decatur House, *Historic American Buildings Survey*

Stairway rising from the second-floor hall to the attic

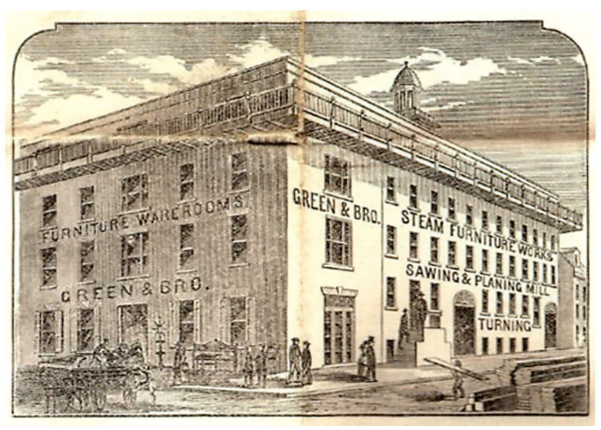

James Green's furniture works, *Courtesy of The Library of Virginia, Ephraim Baker Records, 50152*

TULEYRIES ACCOUNT BOOK ENTRIES

3/30/1835
James Green - Alexandria
1 pair spring seat sofas - $130.00,
1 pair back spring lounges - $90.00,
1 large center table - $45.00,
1 doz. mahogany chairs - $75.00,
1 dressing bureau marble top - $50.00,
1 dressing bureau mahogany top - $30.00,
1 spring seat rocking chair - $15.00,
2 cane seat rocking chairs - $12.00,
1 extra size mahogany bed stead - $35.00,
1 bed stead cornice for ditto - $12.00,
1 pair pier tables marble top - $120.00,
2 Spanish settees - $30.00,
1 easy chair - $18.00,
1 marble wash stand - $17.00,
3 high ? ? for bed stead - $42.00,
1 large mahogany candle stand - $10.00,
1 marble wash stand - $15.00 = $746.00

9/1/1835
John R. Johnston
5 picture frames - $4.00

3/10/1836
James Green - 1 piano stool- $6.00,
1 hat rack - $10.00 = $16.00

3/25/1836
Robert Keyworth - Washington, D. C.
pr. candlelabra - $46.00,
1 silver sugar dish and cream - $71.00,
1 pr coasters - $14.00,
1 doz ?&? forks - $14.00,
1 doz plain forks - $12.00,
1 pr candlesticks - $12.00,
1 snuffer and tray - $4.00 = $173.00

3/26/1836
Robert Keyworth
2 metal? combs - $2.00

7/25/1836
John R. Johnston
9 picture frames - $34.00,
one looking glass plate - $4.50

11/29/1836
Robert Keyworth
1 silver cup - $8.50

3/17/1837
Robert Keyworth
1 silver pitcher - $88.50,
2 plated baskets - $25.00 = $124.00

Mary Tuley's china cup and saucer

Dessert plate of Mary Tuley

From the Colonel's ledger one can get a flavor of the contents of the house during the Tuleys' tenure. Between 1835 and 1837, they purchased numerous furnishings from James Green and silverware from Robert Keyworth in Washington. John R. Johnston provided at least 14 picture frames. James Green was the son of an English cabinetmaker who was advertising in Alexandria by 1820. He had taken over the business, which was located in a building still standing at the corner of Prince and Fairfax Streets. The business continued until 1887 and was known for its customer base in the Shenandoah Valley. Keyworth was located on Pennsylvania Avenue between 9th and 10th Streets and most of his surviving work is dated to the 1830s. He counted Jefferson Davis among his clients. Between the purchases recorded in the Colonel's ledger and what the Colonel and Mrs. Jackson must have had before their marriage, the new house on the Rattle Snake Springs tract must have been well furnished.

Silver ladle by John Peter Latruite

Unfortunately, only three items known to have been owned by them remain in the house. The first is a cup and saucer of gold-rimmed china with Mary W. Tuley's name and Tuleyries, Va. painted in gold on the cup. In the empire style, it must have been part of a much larger set and was obviously ordered specially for the house. Another is a silver ladle, not by the Washington silversmith Keyworth, but marked "I. P. LATRUITE", the work of John Peter Latruite of Alexandria who was advertising his wares as early as 1815. Said to have belonged to Mary Tuley before her marriage to the Colonel, it passed to her cousin, George Whitfield Brown, whose daughter, Errol Cuthbert Train, returned it to The Tuleyries in 1941. The final piece is a dessert plate with a brilliant blue border and a hand-painted bouquet of flowers in the center. Even this limited collection gives a tantalizing taste of the elegance with which Col. and Mary Tuley furnished their home.

While the furnishings of the house have not survived *in situ*, various other additions made shortly after the house was completed do. In 1833, Col. Tuley paid for brick for his stable at the same time he paid for brick for the house. In 1834, he paid William Trenary for "building smoke house and two wings, flue in smoke house." Both of these buildings still stand. The stable was considerably reworked after the turn of the 20th century but the smoke house survives virtually as built although its cupola appears to have been considerably embellished long after the Tuleys departed. The use of the wings on this building is not known but the vents above their doors indicate it was not for curing hams.

In the summer of 1839, the Colonel paid to have his Porter Lodge plastered. This delightful building bears a considerable aesthetic relationship to the entry hall of the house. It serves as a gate house to the lawn which is enclosed by dry-laid stone walls. One drives through the middle of the three arches and could enter on foot through either of those on the sides. Each arch was gated on the outside and there were single 15 feet by 15 feet rooms on either side of the arches. On the outside, each room had a single window set within a relieving arch and on the lawn side, doors were accented with inset arches of similar size to those over the foot passages. The stepped gables on the long sides of the building, echoed in the chimneys on the short sides, may be the first appearance of this element at The Tuleyries and predate those on the 1846 Wickliffe Church and 1847 dependencies at Smithfield. Many more were to follow over the years. The relationship between the Porter Lodge and the entry is such that one is tempted to think that the entry "dome" and arches were added after construction of the house around the same time the lodge was built and might have been the "other plastering" for which the Colonel paid at the time. As unlikely as that may be, the entry is far more akin to this building than anything else in the house. Somewhere along the way, the Tuleys built the picturesque seed house which now anchors one end of the modern garden and decided to add a greenhouse or conservatory to the left rear of the house. All of this had occurred by June 13, 1845, when a remarkable article ran on the front page of the *Richmond Enquirer*. Entitled "A Pleasing Picture," its contemporary description of Col. Tuley's establishment merits repetition in full.

> *In continuing our peregrinations through the rich valley of the Shenandoah, we took occasion on a few days since to visit the residence of Col. Tuley, near Millwood. This estate, from the vast improvements constantly going on, and the peculiar system pursued in the culture of the soil, is esteemed one of the most productive, as well as handsomest, farms in Virginia. There is*

Smoke house with wings

Porter Lodge

upwards of 1200 acres of land, of the best quality of limestone, of which Col. Tuley has some eight or nine hundred in cultivation. The fields are of convenient size, easy of access, and secured with the most substantial fencing we have met with anywhere, and such a high estimate does the Colonel place upon stone wall, that he has about six miles of this species of fencing, representing a strong bulwark to the depredations of animals.

The wheat crop, (of which Col. T. has about 500 acres under cultivation,) is among the very best, as it certainly is the cleanest we have seen in our travels. In looking over the fields, we could not discover a straw of any other kind of grain, or a weed to infest the growth of the wheat. This fact, when we take into consideration the vast quantity in tillage, is worthy of commendation, and must force itself upon the attention of the neighborhood, and influence others to imitate so good an example. Though the drought has been severely felt in this section of the country, yet Col. T.'s land has struggled hard to repay the hand that nurses it. The varieties of wheat sown are, the Genesee white, Georgia, Mediterranean, Golden-straw, and Pennsylvania Red. He has 180 acres in corn, and about 40 acres in oats, which promise a very fair yield. He has also some very fine cattle of the Short-Horn, Devon, and Teeswater breeds, and a small flock of sheep, which he keeps for his own use.

In the cultivation of his farm, Col. T. "pursues what is called 'five years shift system,' and is as follows: He takes a field two years in clover and turns over the sod in the month of August or early in September. From the 5th to the 15th of October, he sows a bushel and a half of wheat to the acre, and harrows it in. After the wheat is cut, the field lies and becomes covered with a thick and strong growth of rag-weed. In the following spring he turns up with a plough, and plants corn before the middle of April. The corn is planted four feet apart each way, and eight or ten kernels in a hill. The cultivation is principally done with a plough, beginning as soon as the corn is fairly up, and ploughing it both ways about four times in the season. At the second ploughing the hoe follows, and the corn is thinned to two stalks in the hill. The hoe is seldom used but once, and the corn is hilled no more than the plough will do it. When the corn is so ripe that it will mature in the stock, it is cut, and the land put into wheat. Sometimes he sows on the seed, and ploughs it in; sometimes he first ploughs, and then sows and harrows in the seed - being governed by the ground. After the wheat is sown, the field is seeded to clover. The field then lies two years in clover, when wheat again follows. In the Spring of each year, half a bushel to an acre of plaster is sown on the clover, and heavy crops of grass are in this way secured. In this course of farming, he once raised from two acres of land 80 bushels of wheat: from a field of 60 acres, he averaged more than 31 bushels to the acre; and 65 bushels of shell corn to the acre. He considers the clover and the plaster as the principal means of improving the soil, yet he is very careful to allow no manure to be wasted. On the contrary, he makes large quantities of it annually, which he applies to the highest parts of fields, turning it under with the plough, which he prefers using as a top dressing."

To pretend to give anything like an accurate description of Col. Tuley's residence, with its tall Corinthian classic columns, or the beautiful order of its architecture, would be subjecting us to a task from which we would shrink, and one better calculated for the painter's pencil than for the editor's pen.

The mansion stands upon a rising knoll, from the observatory of which the eye can survey a vast space of country. The pleasure grounds covering an area of some twelve acres, slope gradually from the house, which, with its fine shrubbery, its beautiful ornamental trees, and the large and rare collection of roses and other flowering plants, present a fascinating appearance, and would woo even a poet from his visionary haunts. In approaching the eastern entrance, you enter through the gateway, with a lodge on either side handsomely constructed which serves the purpose for an ornament to the grounds and also as a convenient hall for servants. The walks and carriage-way are admirably constructed, and we were much pleased with the Gothic Arch formed by the elm tree, leading to the vestibule. Under this arch, Col. T. has erected very handsome pedestals, surmounted with vases, which tend to give the arbor thus formed quite a classic appearance. We also noticed some very fine statuary among this collection of ornaments, not forgetting Ceres, the Goddess of Agriculture, and Flora the Queen of Flowers. There are also arbours on either side of the arch, handsomely festooned with flowers, and surmounted with the statuary of Taglioni and Eilsler [Elssler]; the celebrated dancers.

In the Green House we noticed a large collection of exotics, the fragrance of which, when the folding doors were thrown open, emitted an odor through the rooms, that reminded us of those strange romantic tales which lovers descant so much about and which nine-tenths of them never realize, even in their dreamy imaginations. Col. T. showed us many rare specimens of the rose, the honey-suckle, the Magnolia, the Rose of Sharon and the Lily of the Valley, so beautifully mentioned in Scripture; and Bulrush of the Nile, such as formed the ark of the infant Moses. There we also found the Lemon and Orange tree blooming and bending 'neath the weight of their rich luxurious fruit. There are many more rare plants which we should like to take notice of, but as we must bring our remarks to a close on this subject, we would merely mention here, as in place, the most beautiful flower blooming in this vast collection, is the smiling laughter-loving native, called mine hostess.

Having hastily taken a glance at the residence and pleasure grounds of Col. T., we shall now endeavor to transport the eye of the reader to the fruit and kitchen garden adjacent to the pleasure grounds. Here the Colonel has been most profuse in the cultivation of the various vegetables used on the table. The Garden contains about three acres of ground, closed in with a strong stone wall, some eight feet high. The front wall of brick, with a stone basement, excels anything of the kind we ever saw, and evinces a taste scarcely to be seen in the way of fencing in this country. As we, however, have not time to give a full description of all that is worthy of notice, we shall briefly remark, that we found some fifteen varieties of the strawberry (from the earliest to the latest,) blooming and bearing the most delicious fruit. The raspberry is also growing here very luxuriantly, and of the choicest kinds; and, in fact, all the fruits known to flourish in this country, have been culled with care, and are now maturing under the fostering hand of Col. Tuley. The Garden House next attracted our attention, as being the best constructed we have yet seen. It has a basement sufficiently large for all useful purposes, and admirably adapted for stowing away winter vegetables. The first floor is devoted to garden implements and seeds; and the second story forms a pigeon house, from which Col. T. is daily supplied with the young, tender pigeon. We forgot to mention among the early vegetables, that we saw potatoes growing in this garden fit for table use; and corn almost ready to tassel.

Col. T. has also a park of some 40 acres, enclosed with a high fence, in which he keeps his fallow deer. These beautiful animals supply his table with venison and are much esteemed for the daintiness of their flesh. He has also the Elk and Buffalo grazing on his farm, which are great curiosities to some, and present quite a unique appearance when compared with the domestic animals of the place.

Col. Tuley's "best constructed" Garden House

As comprehensive as this description is, it does not mention the "Ten-Pin Alley, 90 feet long" which was included in a later advertisement. However, the earliest photograph of The Tuleyries dated 1872 does show a single-story greenhouse sitting like the rest of the house atop a raised basement. It projects from the left rear of the house and the wall facing southeast is glazed with pairs of tall 16-pane sash. It is likely that the other three walls were solid brick and that a chimney rose along the long rear wall, creating what would more likely be called a conservatory or orangerie than a greenhouse in the modern sense. When it was connected to the house is impossible to say although the 1845 article says that

1872 photograph showing the "Green House" at left

opening the doors of the greenhouse "emitted an odor through the rooms." It is also interesting to note that the brick appears unpainted, leading to the supposition that the white paint followed later additions to the rear of the house when matching the brick became impossible.

When architect Mantle Fielding drew as-built plans for the house in the early 20th century, the conservatory still existed and what became the library and kitchen and the rooms above them were in place. The inventory filed after Colonel Tuley's death in 1860 clearly shows that they had already been built at that time. Its reference to the drawing room and library must have considered the double parlors as the single drawing room as even in a house as large as The Tuleyries, it would have been impossible to fit "24 hair seat mahogany chairs" into one half of the double parlors.

Transom between rear parlor and library

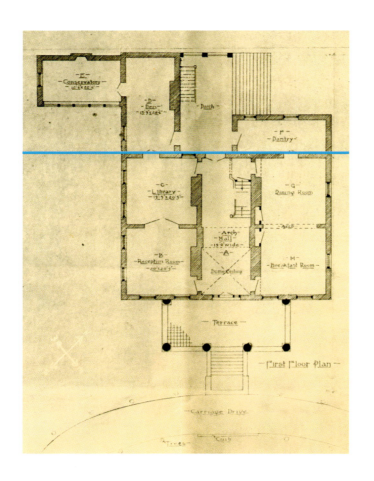

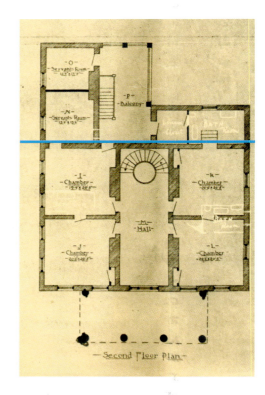

Mantle Fielding's as-built drawings showing extent of original house and later additions

The final clue may be the painted glass transom above the doors which now connect the rear parlor to the library. The rondel with the eagle contains 31 stars. If one assumes those 31 stars represented 31 states, the transom must have been created, if not installed, after the admission of California as the 31st state on September 9, 1850. This window, even if it does not establish a definitive date for the additions to the house, has become the stuff of legend over the years. The story was often told that Union soldiers were about to torch the house when a slave still on the property showed the window to one of them, telling him that the eagle meant the house was Federal property. The soldier is said to have believed this and spared the house. Despite other depredations in the valley, there is no indication that the house was ever under threat of destruction but the story and the window live on.

That the Colonel was able to pay for all of this depended in the first instance on the tanning business he had inherited from his father and to which he added over the years. He purchased a house and tanyard in nearby Paris from David O. Glascock in 1831. From 1840 to 1846, he rented a tanyard in Front Royal from Charles Green. To read the Colonel's ledger is to be amazed that any animal in the Valley of Virginia had a skin at all. In 1839, he hired a gardener, W. Weir, for $14.00 per month who stayed around at least into 1841. Part of Weir's duties seem to have included selling plants. It appears that in addition to farming his own land, Tuley rented the Glenowen farm during this period, a fact which may account for the figure of 1,200 acres in the newspaper article despite Griffith's conclusion that The Tuleyries reached its ultimate size during the Colonel's lifetime of 845 acres in 1849. All of this is said to have led some neighbors to suggest that instead of calling his home The Tuleyries, it should rather be called "Hide Park."

Like the other plantations in the valley and across the South, the basis of Tuley's prosperity was in the final analysis the "peculiar institution" of slavery. In the 1830 census, Col. Tuley is shown as the owner of 53 slaves, of whom 18 were under ten years of age. By 1840, the number had risen to 73, of whom 19 were under ten years of age. The census indicates that 45 of these persons were employed in agriculture while five were employed in manufacture and trade, presumably, the tanning business. The 1850 census lists 37 adult slaves and 28 who were younger than 18. No information was recorded about their employment. The inventory of the Colonel's estate listed 53 slaves in 1860.

All these slaves had to live somewhere and, consistent with his general method of operating his farm and housing his family, he built what must have been one of the most seemingly modern and comfortable accommodations for them anywhere near. Later known as the Barracks, this two-story brick building measures 77 feet by 32 feet including the two-story porch which shades its southeast side and shelters the entry to the ten rooms. Each room had a single door from the porch, one window on the north and south walls and its own fireplace. The windows had jack arches rather than the lintels with corner blocks seen on the main house and the stepped gables incorporated the end chimneys. The most interesting architectural feature is the extended end walls which form the walls of the porch.

A purely utilitarian building laid in common bond, it nonetheless showed considerable attention to detail and symmetry. Its construction is not mentioned in Col. Tuley's ledger and no other information as to its exact date of construction has been located although local historians suggest a date between 1825 and 1830, before construction on the main house began. While it was likely much sturdier than the living quarters of many local freemen, it must have nonetheless been incredibly crowded, especially for families with children, even when the Porter Lodge was also providing housing for slaves.

The southeast front of the Barracks showing the four chimneys and stepped gable ends

The rear of the Barracks showing brick cornice and later addition to the left

In addition to his farming and business activities and duties as colonel in the local militia, Joseph Tuley maintained an ongoing interest in politics. A Jacksonian Democrat, he was among those who signed the initial petition to create Clarke County from Frederick County in 1833. He was appointed to the Democratic Corresponding Committees of Clarke County in 1836, 1840, and 1845. His connections with the Burwells and Nelsons of Long Branch were apparently lifelong. One of the Burwells presented his nomination to become brigadier general of the 16th Brigade to the Virginia House in 1840. Unfortunately, he received the fewest votes of the four nominees, the post being won by Col. James H. Carson of Frederick County who had been nominated by a Mr. Byrd. Frederick County may have lost Clarke County but appears to have maintained its prominence. Like his father before him, the younger Tuley retained an interest in the Ashby's Gap Turnpike Company, serving as a director in 1849.

As noted in the *Richmond Enquirer* article quoted above, Col. Tuley maintained fallow deer, elk, and buffalo at The Tuleyries. He seems to have been interested in these animals from a scientific perspective in addition to their value as ornaments to the landscape and food for the table. He was a corresponding member of the National Institution for the Promotion of Science and in 1842 presented "Antlers of Elk" to the Institution's collection. This donation was followed by "A perfect skin of a large Buck Elk" in 1843 and a "skin of a Female Elk" in 1844. The institution's collection was given to the Smithsonian in 1863 after membership declined but it must have been a very prominent group as the opening address of its 1844 meeting was delivered by President John Tyler.

It is not known if the Colonel attended that meeting but he rented a house in the District during this period and he and Mary are said to have spent much of their winters in the city around this time. There must have been a close connection to Tyler which led to the presence of the Tuleys at two events which were notorious at the time and were carefully recorded. The first involved a cruise on the Potomac arranged to impress the Mexican ambassador General Juan Almonte with the power of a new weapon, a cannon called the Peacemaker. The cruise aboard the USS *Princeton* was an event of the afternoon of February 28, 1844, amid the ongoing national debate concerning the annexation of Texas. All but one of President Tyler's cabinet were on board as well as some five hundred other guests and crew, including the Tuleys. When the Peacemaker, the largest gun mounted on a ship up to that time, was fired the third time in salute to Mount Vernon, it exploded, killing two members of the Cabinet and five others.

The Tuleys, having escaped injury, were not mentioned in the press accounts of the *Princeton* tragedy but their presence is noted in a fascinating book entitled *Court Circles of the Republic* published by subscription in 1867 by Mrs. E. T. (Elizabeth Fries) Ellet, a prolific author credited by some with writing the first historical accounts of women's involvement in the early development and settlement of America. *Court Circles* is described as, "Illustrating life and society under eighteen presidents; describing the social features of the successive administrations from Washington to Grant." Like other books published at the time such as Rice and Hart's 1859 *The National Portrait Gallery*, it contained engravings of its subjects. First ladies Washington, Tyler, and Grant lead a group that are not now generally remembered, including Mary Tuley.

Mrs. Ellet records that the Tuleys attended the farewell ball given by the Tylers at the end of the President's term:

Page 364.

Mrs. Tuley (Virginia) from *Court Circles of the Republic*

At this ball Mrs. Tuley of Virginia was conspicuous and admired. Her dress was elegant, and her ornaments superb and in good taste. Her stately grace and elegance of manner marked her as an appropriate representative of the proud and luxurious 'Old Dominion.' She has for years past been extensively

Railroad station at Boyce, Virginia

THE **B**OYCES

The death of Colonel Joseph Tuley in June of 1860 brought an end to the first glory days of The Tuleyries. The grand estate eventually passed to Col. and Mrs. Upton Boyce but it took a sad and tortuous route to get there, all played out against the background of the Civil War, ultimately leaving Mary Tuley virtually destitute.

Col. Tuley left no will and under the Virginia laws of intestacy, Mary was entitled to one-third of his real estate for life and the rest of his real property passed to his three surviving sisters or their descendants. His sister, Mary Tuley, married Henry Mitchell in 1811. Belinda Tuley married Charles Strother in 1818, and Sarah Tuley married Uriel Wright in 1827. The Colonel's widow sold her one-third life interest in the Colonel's estate in October following his death to Mary Mitchell, Uriel Wright, Charles Strother and Joseph T. Strother.

Mary Tuley Mitchell and her husband, Henry, lived at La Grange in Augusta County, property she inherited from her father. Belinda Tuley Strother died before her brother and her interest passed to Joseph T. Strother and Charles Strother. The Strothers, like every other Southern family, used the same three names over and over again so it is not clear exactly who these two gentlemen were. Charles may have been Belinda's husband, her son, or he may have been the husband of her daughter Abby who married a cousin by the same name. Joseph T. may have been Belinda's son or the son of her son Charles. Regardless, an 1846 letter transcribed by Griffith from Joseph T. Strother to his uncle, Colonel Tuley, was posted from Pointe Coupée Parish, Louisiana. A reference in the New Orleans *Crescent* from July, 1857 refers to Joseph T. Strother as the "proprietor of the magnificent hotel known as the Morganza Hotel, and also adjoining buildings." Morganza, a small town on the Mississippi River between Baton Rouge and Natchez, today boasts no building which could be described as magnificent but there are Strothers all over Louisiana.

In 1827, Sarah Tuley married Uriel Sebree Wright, a native of nearby Madison County, Virginia. Born in 1804, Wright was accepted at West Point in 1819 and spent two years there before acceding to his father's wishes that he study law. This he did in Winchester where he was admitted to the bar and practiced until removing to Missouri in 1833. He quickly established himself in Palmyra and by 1836 had been elected to the state legislature. Noted as a great orator and renowned criminal defense lawyer, he was somewhat less successful in business, having invested heavily in a new town along the Mississippi which was washed away in the flood of 1844. This prompted him to move to St. Louis where he eventually practiced law with his son-in-law, Upton Lawrence Boyce.

In the lead-up to the Civil War, Wright was a staunch opponent of secession. On February 10, 1858, while the strife of Bleeding Kansas was in full swing, he wrote to Colonel Tuley a four-page letter which first reported family news but by the third page launched into an extended commentary on the political situation in both Kansas and Washington.

> *As you are near the Capitol, and are one of the "people" - I trust you will not let the demagogues and tricksters of Washington dissolve the Union before spring. - I am for dissolving Congress - Cabinet and President - after ceding back Kansas to the Indians, who were better governors of that territory than we have proven ourselves to be. -*
>
> *Kansas + Nebraska, has turned out to be only a Grecian horse - where cavernous sides were filled with criminal men - . Both parties in Kansas have for years been playing at cheat and it is impossible to decide which has been most skilful at fraud.*
>
> *There has not been one honest fair election in that territory from the first to the last. Law, has never prevailed in it one day. - We know it true - and hence every reasonable man is thoroughly disgusted at the mention of Kansas.*
>
> *It is a nut to the politicians and a calamity to the country.*
>
> *If I were in Congress - I should gravely and solemnly propose to recede the territory to the Red Man.*
>
> *Either that - or Andrew Jackson. Jackson always said Buchanan had no nerve + was a trimmer. He almost weeps (in his last message) over the dissolution of the Union. - I repeat with Crittenden - "I thank God it is not in the power of President or Congress or both to break up this Union." -*
>
> *Kansas began as electioneering capital - Kansas is now nothing else - Democrats and Republicans - both use it to consolidate party power. The country is not the concern.*

Consistent with his view expressed to Col. Tuley, Wright was elected to the Missouri state constitutional convention of 1861 as an "Unconditional Union" man. However, after Union troops killed some 28 civilians in the streets of St. Louis in May of that year, an event later known as the Camp Jackson massacre, he changed allegiance and served as an officer on the staffs of Confederate generals Price and Van Dorn, achieving the rank of major. It is unclear whether he returned to St. Louis after the war or settled in Winchester directly. Regardless, he was soon back in Virginia where he died in 1869. Nothing more is known about Sarah except her dates of birth in 1804, marriage in 1827, and death in November 1861, and that she was the mother of eight children, six of whom died as infants. She and her husband apparently maintained close ties with Joseph and Mary Tuley, the latter referring to Sarah as "Sister Wright" in a letter she wrote in 1839 which noted that the Wrights were then staying at The Tuleyries which was "a great pleasure to us all."

The two children of the Wrights who lived to adulthood were their daughter, Belinda, named for her aunt, and Joseph Tuley Wright, named for his grandfather and uncle, who later lived in Point Christian, Mississippi. Belinda married Upton Lawrence Boyce in 1858. Boyce was born in Greenup County, Kentucky, in 1830, into a family which originally hailed from Surry County, Virginia. He later continued its westward migration, moving to Missouri. It is not recorded where he read law but by 1858, he had become a good friend of Uriel Wright, practiced law with him, and married his daughter. A transcribed copy of Boyce's obituary states that he became an "intimate friend" of U. S. Grant who, from 1854 to 1859 was seeking to make a living as a farmer on property near St. Louis. From this, one would assume that Boyce, like his father-in-law, was a staunch supporter of the Union. However, whether due to Wright's influence or his own reaction to Union activities in St. Louis, he served during the Civil War in the Clarke Cavalry, Sixth Virginia Regiment, CSA, and used the title Colonel for the rest of his days.

After the war Boyce, like Wright, settled into law practice in Winchester. One can only assume that Sarah Wright's one-third interest in The Tuleyries following the Colonel's death was an enticement for the return. R. E. Griffith's 1936 research states that the Boyces were living at The Tuleyries by 1866.

Meanwhile, Mary Tuley had been left to deal with her husband's estate and the Civil War. As he had died intestate, she was appointed administratrix of the estate at the August term of 1860. She sold her one-third life interest in her husband's real estate to his heirs in a deed dated October 5, 1860. Consideration for her interest was stated as $12,000. The heirs must have been eager to convert the estate into cash as Mary's nephew, Joseph Tuley Mitchell, immediately advertised an auction at which it, along with houses in Winchester and White Post, and his grandfather's house and tanyard in Millwood, would be offered for sale. The advertisements which ran in the Alexandria and Staunton newspapers contain the rather remarkable introduction which begins, "Having succeeded at last in purchasing the dower right of the widow of Joseph Tuley, dec'd... ." Given that the Colonel had not yet been dead four months, Mary can hardly have been accused of dragging her feet in deciding what to do with her interest in the estate.

These ads were signed by "Jos. T. Mitchell, Agent and Attorney in fact for the Heirs." In the *Alexandria Gazette*, Joseph's ad was followed by one placed by Mary advertising sale of the Colonel's personal property. Both sales were held on October 30, 1860, and Griffith reports that Mary's sale continued for 15 days before being postponed. On November 17, *The Clarke County Journal* reported that the "improvements, with 500 acres of land were bought by Mr. Simonton, of Baltimore, for $72½ per acre. Some 400 acres were bought by Mr. John Alexander, at $60 per acre for a portion of it." This would have amounted to $60,250, not counting the other houses and the tanyard. Something happened and the sales did not go through. Possibly the election of Republican Abraham Lincoln as president a week after the sale gave the buyers cold feet. Whatever the reason may have been, on November 22 the following notice ran in the *Clarke Conservator*: "We are requested to state that the 'Tuleyries' Farm has not been sold to Mr. Simonton, of Baltimore, or to any one else, as has been lately reported."

Those who purchased property at either auction were allowed to pay over time and to tender notes for their debts. As Mary Tuley's attorney stated in a pleading in *Mary W. Tuley, Admtrx. v. Joseph T. Thomas, Exor. et al.*, litigation which was still pending almost twenty years later:

AUCTION SALES.

"TULEYRIES" FOR SALE.—Having succeeded at last in purchasing the dower-right of the widow of Joseph Tuley, dec'd, I will offer for sale, to the highest bidder, on *Tuesday, the 30th day of October,* 1860, on the premises, that highly valuable estate known as the "TULEYRIES," the late residence of Col. Joseph Tuley, dec'd., in the county of Clarke, State of Virginia. This elegant and magnificent estate contains 869 ACRES of fine land, in a high state of cultivation, with valuable improvements, consisting of an elegant and commodious MANSION HOUSE, lighted with gas in every room; out-houses of brick, substantially built, and comprise a Gas House, large Dairy, Ten-Pin Alley 90 feet long, Carriage House and two Stables attached, Porter Lodge, Ice House, and all other necessary out-buildings, of the best kind. There is within thirty yards of the Mansion an elegant Artesian Well of never failing water, and the Garden of 4 acres is surrounded with a substantial Stone and Brick Wall 8 feet high. The improvements on the estate, in point of style, elegance and durability, cannot be surpassed by any in the State of Virginia. There are about 700 acres of this tract enclosed and divided entirely by a neat Stone Fence of the best kind. In short, the "TULEYRIES," as a country residence, is well known as the Garden Spot of the United States.

There is on the farm an OVERSEER'S HOUSE, an elegant Brick Quarter, 20 feet wide and 80 feet long, a large Barn, Stables, Corn House; Blacksmith Shop, and all necessary out-buildings, suitable on such an estate. There will be 425 acres seeded in wheat by the 12th of this month, (October,) and if a favorable season in the Spring, will average about 20 to 30 bushels of wheat to the acre.

The property will be shown to persons desiring to see it by Joseph T. Mitchell, and letters addressed to him at Millwood, Clarke County, Va., will be attended to.

I will also sell, at the same time and place, a good BRICK HOUSE and LOT, in Winchester, known as the residence of the late Judge White. It has 2 acres of land attached to the Mansion, which will make a very desirable residence to the purchaser. It is about five or six squares from the Court House.

At the same time, I will sell one of the best TAN-YARDS in this section of the State, containing about 4 acres of land, with a delightful HOUSE covered with Tin, lying in the village of Millwood. Any judicious and enterprising person can, as has been done, make a snug fortune in a short time, as the surrounding neighborhood is wealthy.

Also, I will sell a HOUSE and LOT, containing 1½ acres of land, lying in the centre of the village of White Post. Also, a very desirable LOT in the town of Paris, in the county of Fauquier.

I will also sell, at the same time and place, 63 NEGROES, comprising mechanics, House Carpenters, and Farm Hands—an unusually likely, young and valuable lot of NEGROES, seldom offered for sale in any community.

There will also be sold, at the same time and place, all the PERSONAL PROPERTY belonging to the said estate, consisting of 32 Horses and Mules, Stock of every kind, Wheat, Cloverseed, and all kinds of Farming Implements, HOUSEHOLD FURNITURE of a superior kind, and other valuable property too tedious to mention. Also, 77 head of English Fallow Deer, which are superior to the Mountain Deer in every respect.

TERMS OF SALE:—For the Real Estate, one-fourth in hand, and the residue in three equal annual payments, with interest from the day of sale, and the title to be retained until the whole purchase money is paid. For the Negroes, cash, or a Negotiable Note at thirty days, well endorsed, with interest added. For the Personal Property, terms as usual.

The sale will be continued from day to day until concluded.   JOS. T. MITCHELL.
Agent and Attorney in fact for the Heirs.
TURK & CUSHING, Auctioneers.
Clarke county, oct 9—eotd

PUBLIC SALE.—I will, on *Tuesday, 30th day of October,* 1860, sell, at public sale, all the vendible personal estate, (except the slaves) of Col. Joseph Tuley, dec'd., at "TULEYRIES," his late residence in the county of Clarke, embracing, amongst others, the following subjects, to wit: A large quantity of valuable HOUSEHOLD and KITCHEN FURNITURE, including every description. Also, the farm stock, comprising fifteen horses, twelve mules, and 5 horse and mule Colts, fifty-six head of cattle, including a number of valuable oxen; 95 head of hogs, large and small; 87 head of sheep, large and small; about seventy-five deer and one elk; a large quantity of machinery, comprising three Wheat Reapers, 4 Drills, 1 Threshing Machine, 2 Clover Hullers, 3 Wheat Fans, 1 Cider Press, Corn Shellers, &c. Also, Farming Utensils, embracing a very large quantity of every description, usually found upon estates of the kind, including a quantity of Gear. Blacksmith's Tools, comprising a full sett; Grain of various kinds, including the crop of wheat of the last harvest, estimated to amount to four thousand five hundred bushels. About 100 barrels of old corn; 93 acres of corn in the field; a quantity of oats, buckwheat, cloverseed, &c. Two family Carriages, 1 Buggy, with Harness, &c., for each. Also, four Coupon Bonds of the State of Virginia, two of $5,000 each, and two of $1,000 each; 10 shares of Valley Bank Stock; 50 shares of Winchester and Potomac Railroad Stock; 112 do. of Ashby's Gap Turnpike Stock; 4 do. of Winchester and Berry's Ferry Turnpike Stock.

TERMS OF SALE:—In respect of said Wheat, Coupon Bonds and Bank Stock, a credit of 90 days—on the purchaser giving a negotiable note, satisfactorily endorsed. In respect of all other subjects, a credit of nine months, but with interest from date, (the interest, however, to be remitted, if the amount should be paid at maturity) on the purchaser giving bond with approved security, on all purchases which may exceed five dollars. For amounts under that sum, the cash will be required. The interest which has accrued on the Coupon Bonds will be added on. No articles to be removed until said terms are complied with. As to the Grain, it will be made known on the day of sale in what form it will be sold.
MARY W. TULEY,
Administratrix of Col. Joseph Tuley, dec'd.
Clarke County, Va., oct 13—2aw5t

Auction notices advertising the sale of The Tuleyries and its contents run in the Alexandria and Staunton papers in October and November 1860

44

> [Joseph Tuley] was to some extent indebted, and some considerable debts were owing to him. ... In October 30 of the same year [1860] she proceeded to sell the property and hire the slaves, which had belonged to her said husband. In a few months thereafter the Civil War broke out and during its pendency she had no opportunity to settle her accounts nor could she enforce collection of debts owing to the estate, or of the sale bills taken by her. ... By reference to said [Commissioner's] report it will be seen that your oratrix was therein charged with the whole amount of the sales, altho' a very small part thereof had at that time been collected: but whilst then stating the account, the commissioner mentioned in his said report, that from the condition of the Country, collections could not have been made, and that she would be entitled in a future settlement to have credit for all such sums as she might be unable to collect after using due diligence so to do. She here answers that she has used all reasonable diligence to collect the sums owing to the estate, but very many of them, together making a considerable amount yet remain unpaid, and she fears must be regarded as entirely lost.

In the same pleading Mary went on to say that various persons entitled to receive property from her husband's estate also owed it money and sought set-off for these amounts. She also noted that she had not yet been paid all of the $12,000 for her life interest which had "finally" been sold to the heirs in October of 1860.

While Joseph Tuley Mitchell had advertised the Colonel's slaves for sale in the October 1860 auction notice, they were either not offered for sale or had no buyers. Twenty years after the fact, Mary Tuley testified at a deposition concerning their disposition:

> In the Spring of 1863 Barton and Williams [Winchester attorneys], or one of them, I think Mr. Barton advised me to send the servants those belonging to the heirs that there was some contention about to send them up the valley to keep them from going off with the Federal Army saying if I did not do so, the heirs might attempt to make me responsible for them, this was as severe and a most troublesome undertaking for me to do alone without any assistance from any one, I fortunately knew Major Melton from South Carolina Quarter master he kindly offered me his assistance I finally got them all together and Col. Melton took charge of them to Richmond and put them in the hands of the principal auctioneer (his name I now do not remember) who hired them out sometime after I went to Richmond to look after them they wandered about and left their places most of them had returned home and rather wandering about home, of course I had no control over them... . (Quoted from R. E. Griffith transcription, 1936.)

A much more personal version of this sad story was told by Mary Tuley in an April 1883 letter believed to have been sent to George Whitfield Brown. She signs the letter Aunt Tuley but the exact connection is obscure. George's grandmother was Elizabeth Reilly Brown who was Mrs. Jackson before she became Mrs. Brown. Another of George's aunts was his father's sister Mary Elizabeth who married John Hill Wheeler, a North Carolina native.

Mary Elizabeth was staying at The Tuleyries at the time of her death in 1836 and is buried at Old Chapel. Remembering that Aunt Tuley was first married to Dr. Jackson and that her middle name was Wheeler, one is nonetheless at a loss to know exactly how George connected but he was clearly close to Mary Tuley who poured her heart out to him.

> *My estate before the war was at least fifty thousand dollars, I had one half of my husband's personal property and a third in his real estate, all free from debt or care - I was offered twenty five thousand dollars for my servants that fell to me in the division of the slaves, but I refused it as they were not willing to leave me + in 18 months they were all liberated &c. I sold my real estate to the Heirs and as they had no money to pay me, I took bonds which were considered good and satisfactory.*
>
> *The War came on, and for nearly five years no business was transacted, no Courts in Session, all the plantations sacked of everything, on many of the plantations the buildings were all burnt by the order of Genl Hunter of Washington, and Gel Sheridan before he left the Valley he sent his scouts out for many miles around Winchester, + had all the grain burnt up, saying we should all perish + if the Rebels ever got back here again they should have nothing to eat &c - of course I shared largely in this awful destruction they burnt at Tuleyries 15 thousand bushels of wheat half of it mine.*
>
> *After the war there was a law made by the Federal Government that no one should be forced or made to pay their debts for three years*
>
> *Then came the Bankrupt which was also dishonest that taken by large numbers. I shared largely in all these acts which robbed me of a very large portion of my means, there is large amount still due me I trust I will get it You will excuse me dear George going into all this worry + trouble relating it to you, I yet have means but I have to be very economical, in consequence of very heavy losses &c as I stated*

All of this occurred against the backdrop of what became known in Civil War lore as the Valley Campaigns of 1862 and 1864. Winchester, then the most important city in the valley, changed hands many times - some said twenty, others as many as seventy. Confederate forces in the valley were led by Stonewall Jackson during the 1862 campaign. Winchester and the route from the valley to Washington were the major points of contention. The Battle of Kernstown was fought on March 23, 1862, some three miles south of Winchester. Said to have been Jackson's only tactical defeat, it prompted Lincoln to divert thousands of troops to the valley who had been marching toward Richmond. On May 23, Jackson with some three thousand men engaged and defeated a smaller Union army at Front Royal, some twelve miles south of White Post. This was a prelude to the Second Battle of Winchester, fought two days later and Jackson's troops must have passed within shouting distance of The Tuleyries on their way north. In that battle, Winchester was again taken by the Confederates. Although there were other engagements near Harrisonburg later that summer, the action moved elsewhere.

At the beginning of the spring of 1864, the campaign in the valley was focused on the rail and telegraph facilities in the upper-southern portion of the valley. In early July,

Confederate general Jubal Early led his troops from Winchester toward Washington, successfully overcoming resistance in the Battle of Monocacy, near Frederick, Maryland, on July 9. He reached Fort Stevens, inside the District near what is now Rock Creek Park, on July 11. Convinced he could not hold, even if he took the fort, Early withdrew on July 13. Union troops followed Early back toward Winchester and a second battle was fought at Kernstown on July 24 in which Early forced the withdrawal of Union troops to Harper's Ferry.

On August 6, in what would prove to be a fateful event for the valley, Lieutenant General Philip Sheridan was assigned command of what became known as the Army of the Shenandoah. The competing armies engaged in various skirmishes throughout August, including one at Double Toll Gate on August 11, just two miles west of White Post. On September 3, some 16,000 Union and 8,000 Confederate forces faced off at Berryville but after an initial attack by Confederate General R. H. Anderson, General Early withdrew. All of this culminated in the Third Battle of Winchester on September 19. In the single day of fighting, Sheridan lost 5,000 men and Early lost 3,500. The percentages however told the story: Sheridan lost 12% of his troops while Early lost 25% of his.

As Sheridan pursued Early up the valley, he ordered what is still remembered as "The Burning." In the wake of Early's raid on Washington, General Grant had ordered Union troops to make the Shenandoah Valley so desolate "that crows flying over it for the balance of the season will have to carry their own provender with them." He later told Sheridan, "If the war is to last another year we want the Shenandoah Valley to remain a barren waste." Beginning in Staunton, Sheridan later claimed that, in addition to thousands of head of livestock slaughtered, he had been responsible for burning "2,000 barns filled with wheat, hay and farming implements [and] over seventy mills filled with flour and wheat." While the story about the transom saving the house from destruction is almost certainly apocryphal, Mary Tuley's lament over the burned wheat is borne out by Sheridan's own boast.

General Early made his last attempt to defeat Sheridan at Cedar Creek, near Belle Grove, the Hite family plantation once the home of James Madison's sister, some ten or twelve miles southeast of White Post. His surprise attack on Sheridan's forces on October 19 was initially successful. However, Sheridan, having been away in Winchester, returned to his troops that afternoon and launched a counterattack which caused the Confederate lines to crumble. A massive battle with more than 30,000 Union and 20,000 Confederate soldiers, it ended Confederate hopes of controlling the Shenandoah Valley for good.

If the fighting near The Tuleyries caused Mary Tuley to move to Winchester by 1863, she jumped from the frying pan into the fire. She was nonetheless a supporter of the cause, purchasing at least one Confederate $2,000 war bond in October 1862. This proved to be a poor investment and just one more financial misfortune which beset her until the end of her days in a situation which reads like Charles Dickens' classic never-ending lawsuit, *Jarndyce v. Jarndyce*. Perhaps the most amazing part of her story from a modern perspective was the role played by various family members and lawyers over the years. But one example involved money borrowed by Sarah Wright from Col. Tuley before his death. Sarah had died in 1861 in Missouri but her husband and son-in-law, Messrs. Wright and Boyce, were both practicing law in Winchester when in 1867 Mary was told by her Virginia lawyer that she would have to hire counsel in Missouri to collect the debt. Later, she nonetheless used Wright and Boyce to collect other debts.

Griffith reports the Boyces were in residence at The Tuleyries by 1866 and Joseph

Mary Tuley's home at 126 North Cameron Street in Winchester, *courtesy of the Handley Regional Library, Winchester, Virginia, Stewart Bell Jr. Archives Room, C. Fred Barr Collection*

Tuley Wright may have lived there after Mary moved to Winchester. The heirs appear to have given up on the idea of selling the plantation as a whole and sometime prior to 1873, the impatient Joseph T. Mitchell filed a suit in the Circuit Court of Clarke County to have the Colonel's lands partitioned. In May of that year, the division was confirmed by the court and 213 (or 204) acres and the mansion house were allocated to Belinda Boyce and her brother, Joseph Tuley Wright, as the heirs of their mother, Sarah Tuley Wright. The siblings worked out their own division and in September 1873, Joseph conveyed to Belinda his interest in the 42 acres and "all buildings and improvements thereon." One assumes that this is the first time that the Boyces became sole owners of any part of The Tuleyries. This deed also refers to another from the Boyces to Wright conveying their interest in the remaining 162 acres of Sarah Wright's portion of the estate. This is the land purchased by Belinda Boyce in 1893 from special commissioners in later litigation with her brother.

Colonel Boyce had been purchasing the interests of other heirs along the way. In November 1866, he purchased a one-ninth interest in the estate from Charles Henry and Abbie O. Strother. This transaction illustrates the difficulty in tracking exactly who did what and with what to whom in this process and in fact when it was done. The deed was held pending payment of notes or court orders arising from litigation when notes were not paid. This one was not filed until June 25, 1879. In 1874, the matter of *Strother, et al. v. Boyce, et*

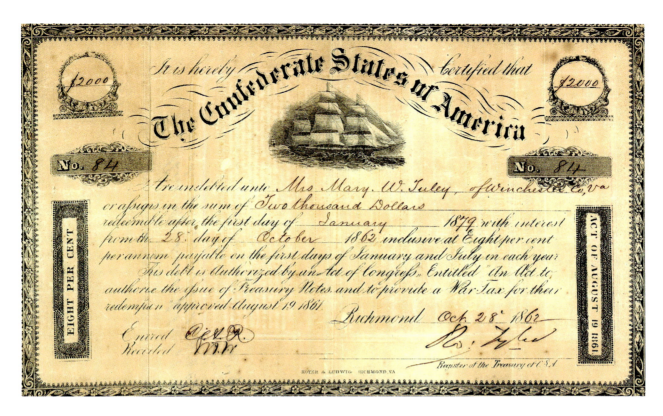

1862 Confederate bond bearing eight percent and maturing in January 1879

al. was filed, apparently seeking to collect some or all of the consideration Upton Boyce had given for the purchase of the remaining interests. As a result of this litigation, Upton's life interest as Belinda's husband in the mansion house and 42 acres and his fee in two other tracts of 262 acres and 211 acres were sold at public auction by order of court on October 18, 1879. A deed conveying this property to Belinda was executed by the commissioner a year later and yet another year later, was recorded on November 16, 1883. Through inheritance and purchase, Belinda Boyce, Colonel Tuley's niece, ultimately held an estate of some 849 acres.

The Boyces are said to have undertaken repairs to The Tuleyries upon taking up residence to erase the scars of the war and to accommodate their family. They had brought their first son, Uriel Wright Boyce, with them to The Tuleyries. He had been born in St. Louis in 1859 and named for his grandfather. After the move to Virginia, daughters Sarah Goen Tuley Wright Boyce, given her grandmother's full married name, was born in 1866, and Katherine Lawrence Shreve Boyce Jones was born in 1868. The 1870s brought two more sons, Upton Lawrence Boyce, named for his father and born in 1873, and William Truxton Boyce, born in 1876. Sarah, despite of or perhaps because of her many names, was known as Sallie and appears not to have married, dying in 1890. Katherine married Robert L. Jones and died in Texas in 1893 shortly after the birth of her son, Upton Lawrence Jones. All three sons married and had children and William's son, Truxton, became the family genealogist, leaving some 26 binders of research materials to the University of Delaware at his death in 2007.

Long-cherished tradition holds that the Boyces purchased various furnishings, including two rosewood etageres, from the sale of the contents of the White House of the

Etagere purchased by Colonel Boyce from the Virginia Governor's Mansion in 1882, *courtesy of the American Civil War Museum, The White House of the Confederacy*

Confederacy. Like so many traditions, this one is off by several years. The White House of the Confederacy or Davis Mansion, had been purchased by the City of Richmond in 1861 to serve as the executive mansion for the Confederacy. Jefferson and Varina Davis lived there until fleeing the city. It was seized by Union forces on April 3, 1865, and used as headquarters for the military district until its return to the city in 1870. By October of that year, the city, no longer needing an executive mansion for the Confederacy, advertised the house and contents for auction. On October 6, it also ran an ad notifying "All persons having in their possession FURNITURE, BOOKS, or other property belonging to the Davis Mansion, hereby notified to return the same." The ad for the sale of the contents listed among other things, "Handsome Rosewood Etegres (sic)." It has long been believed that the pair of etageres that resided at The Tuleyries for more than a hundred years were the pair listed in this ad.

It is possible that the "Etegres" from the Davis Mansion made their way to the Governor's Mansion from the 1870 sale. However, they came to The Tuleyries after being purchased in 1882 at an auction of the contents of the Virginia Governor's Mansion. A letter to later owner Graham Blandy from Colonel Boyce's son, U. Lawrence Boyce, dated June 30, 1920, states that the furniture "came from the Governor's mansion at Richmond Virginia + was purchased by my father. The sale took place as I was informed during Billy Mahone Days in Va. political history known as Readjuster administration." An article in the *Richmond Dispatch* from January 6, 1882, headed "Readjuster Reform" reads in part that, "The entire household and kitchen furniture at the Governor's mansion will be sold at public auction on Monday next. The house is to be thoroughly repaired, repainted, and refurnished before Governor Cameron occupies it." *The Norfolk Virginian* reported on the sale in its January 12, 1882, edition that, "Nearly all of the most valuable furniture was purchased by Mr. U. L. Boyce, the vice-president of the Shenandoah Valley Railroad."

It is unknown whether Boyce had a connection to the Readjusters or simply saw an advertisement of the sale. He certainly would have been aware of Little Billy Mahone, their leader. Mahone was a former Confederate general who after the war, sought to make his fortune in railroads and politics. He succeeded for a while in politics by uniting poor whites and newly enfranchised blacks in a party seeking to repudiate or "readjust" some of Virginia's heavy war debt, enabling it to provide services such as public education to its citizens. The Readjuster Party elected Governor Cameron and sent Mahone to the U. S. Senate in 1881. However, he served only one term before conservative interests in the state again obtained the upper hand.

A date of 1882 for the purchase of the furniture from Richmond is more in line with the Boyces' circumstances and also changes the family made in the house. Their most ambitious project was the conversion of the two rooms to the right of the hall on the first floor into one large room. They replaced the wall between them with a broad arch and paneled the walls halfway up with mahogany to match the original doors which they retained. Massive overmantels with mirrors and shelves for ornaments replaced the original mantels. Mahogany beams were also added to the ceiling giving the now massive room a baronial feeling. Whether the corner cabinet in the northwest corner of the room was inherited or purchased, the Boyces clearly intended for it to remain in its place forever as the walls were not paneled behind it. As a result, it remains there to this day. In the grand double parlors, the Boyces limited themselves to adding new center medallions to the ceilings. They were obviously very proud of their home as evidenced by a silver pitcher which survives at the house today. It not only sports the family name but, like Mary Tuley's cup and saucer, also

Dining or ballroom as remodeled by the Boyces

has the name of the house engraved in the cartouche. To modern eyes, it is a blessing that the Boyces made no other changes to the house but their work adds to the mix of styles that makes The Tuleyries such a fascinating place.

Colonel Boyce seems to have paid for all of this as a result of his efforts on behalf of the Shenandoah Valley Railroad Company. The history of his involvement with this enterprise seems to have been embellished along the way much like the origin of the etageres. After the warring troops left the Shenandoah Valley in 1865, it again became the center of an extended battle waged ultimately by the business interests of Philadelphia, Baltimore, and Norfolk, each of which wished to be the primary port for shipping the coal, iron, and timber which were being exploited in the mountains to the west. To direct traffic to either Philadelphia or Baltimore, a railroad through the valley was deemed essential. Hence by 1867, the Virginia legislature authorized the incorporation of the Shenandoah Valley Railroad Company, the goal of which was to construct a line from Hagerstown, Maryland, to Roanoke, Virginia, through the valley. The legislatures of Maryland and West Virginia authorized the portions of the project in their jurisdictions in 1870 and the company began its existence in that year.

The Pennsylvania Railroad and Norfolk & Western vied for control of this line while the Baltimore & Ohio championed the competing Valley Line with the early assistance of Robert E. Lee. Initial capital for the project came from the Pennsylvania Railroad and the first president of the Shenandoah was Col. Thomas A. Scott who was also a vice president of the Pennsylvania. The latter continued to purchase stock in the new company after it was hit by the financial panic of 1873 and controlled the Central Improvement Co. which was chosen to construct the line. In 1882, the year the line was completed, it had to seek financing from the Philadelphia firm, E. W. Clark & Co., to cover an operating shortfall. Also in that year, the Pennsylvania Railroad took Norfolk & Western stock for its interest in the line. Further infusions of capital failed to make the line profitable and it was operated by a receiver from 1885 until 1890 when it was purchased in full by the Norfolk & Western.

Colonel Boyce was clearly in the thick of these various machinations from at least 1872 until the Shenandoah Valley Railroad was finally subsumed by Norfolk & Western and renamed the Shenandoah Valley Railway in 1890. He was a director of the corporation from 1872 until 1875 when he resigned. The next year he was again elected as a director and became vice president. In 1878, construction was about to collapse and Boyce obtained release of $100,000 from bonds issued by Clarke County. In 1878, Boyce's brother-in-law,

Parlor ceiling medallion

Joseph Tuley Wright, was appointed secretary of the corporation. The line reached Berryville and Millwood in 1879.

In 1881, he was involved in the acquisition of Little Billy Mahone's Atlantic, Mississippi & Ohio Railroad by interests aligned with the Shenandoah and that line was renamed the Norfolk & Western. That year also saw the first train pass from Hagerstown to Waynesboro. Boyce successfully argued that it was essential to connect the Shenandoah with the new Norfolk & Western and in 1883 he became a director of that line. He was part of the syndicate which purchased the Washington, Cincinnati & St. Louis Railroad in 1883.

The recession of 1883 led to the demise of the Shenandoah as an independent entity. By March of 1884, it was running a deficit and it was declared insolvent in April of 1885. Sydney F. Tyler was appointed president and receiver and all other officers resigned except Boyce who remained as vice president. Boyce's involvement finally came to an end in September 1896 when a new version of the Norfolk & Western purchased the line in foreclosure and he retired. On occasion, he appeared in court for one or another of the railroads with which he was involved. Seeking to take advantage of the coming of rail transportation to the valley, he became a director of the Luray Cave Company, organized with the goal of buying the cave and constructing a hotel nearby. He apparently had mechanical abilities as well as a talent for boosterism. In 1885, he received a patent for a thill coupling, a connection between the axle and thill, the apparatus which allowed one rail car to be attached to another.

One story of the Colonel's exploits relayed in the first volume of Stuart Brown's *Annals of Clarke County Virginia* tells that the president of the Pennsylvania Railroad told Boyce that he would give him $50,000 if he got the line "on its feet." After the first train passed over the first section of completed track, Boyce claimed his reward and some say that this was used to acquire the lands of the other heirs of Colonel Tuley. An obituary from *The Clarke Courier* credited Boyce as being "largely instrumental" in construction of the Shenandoah line. There is no doubt that the town of Boyce - originally Boyceville - carries his name in honor of his work bringing the railroad to the valley as did its third locomotive. The first locomotive was named Fairfax in honor of Lord Fairfax and carried a bell from his estate, Greenway Court, which Boyce had bought at auction.

After the insolvency of the Shenandoah in 1885, Boyce appears to have "rested his oars as a farmer and engaged in very little legal business, except a few large cases, in which he had some interest" as related in his *Clarke Courier* obituary. In 1889, the president of the Penn Bank of Pittsburgh obtained a judgment against him for $320,000 alleging that Boyce had not paid fees owed for obtaining financing for the Shenandoah. In 1893, Boyce obtained a $100,000 judgment against the West Virginia Coal and Iron Company. In 1894, *The Norfolk Landmark* reported that he had just won a $200,000 judgment against an unnamed party. That article concluded by reporting that, "He wears a big fairy stone in his cravat, one on his watch charm, has two big ones for cuff buttons, three for shirt studs, and carries several in his pocket for luck. He firmly believes that the stones won his lawsuit and would not go a mile from home without some around his clothes." As the newspapers were better at reporting about judgments than about efforts to collect them, it is unclear if the fairy stones, unusual crystals in the form of a cross found along the Blue Ridge, brought anyone any money. However, the picture painted by the article complements the image of the Colonel in the surviving photograph of him.

Boyce was not the only one engaged in continuing litigation. From the time of Col.

1879 Shenandoah Valley Railroad Company stock certificate attested by Joseph Tuley Wright

Tuley's death until the mid-1880s, Mary Tuley had been plaintiff and defendant in a plethora of litigation seeking to collect moneys owed the Colonel's estate and defend claims made by various of his heirs. In 1874, she was a creditor in the bankruptcy of T. J. Kerfoot. In 1882, she lost a case seeking payment for the sale of Lucky Hit, a portion of The Tuleyries estate. In 1884, her cases against R. T. Burton and David W. Barton were both in the Court of Appeals. Along the way, it seems that all of Colonel Tuley's heirs were suing each other and Mary. In 1884, the Court of Appeals also heard *Wright v. Strother, Wright v. Wright, Boyce v. Strother, Strother v. Xaupi*, and *Xaupi v. Mitchell*. Mary Tuley does not appear to have fared well in any of these actions. In 1885, her daughter, Mary Tuley Jackson, wrote of the situation to George Whitfield Brown.

My Dear George I write to you in a great deal of trouble and distress. For several years a suit has been going on about the house we purchased many years ago. It has been decided against us most unjustly. We have already paid Seven Thousand dollars on it and paid taxes and insurance upon it for twenty years. The cause of the trouble is this, Mama had made all the payments and was owing about two thousand upon it. She put a note to bring suit upon into a lawyer's hands. The man she bought the house from which if he gained it would more than pay what she was owing on the house. He received the note for that purpose. In 1875 he gained the suit and announced in the Courtroom that the money was paid him as Mrs Tuley's attorney and informed Mama so. This was in 1875 and we thought until two or three years ago was all right, but he then informed us that he had not received the money but took a note instead. The man he gained the suit from was very rich at the time and for several years after, but became a bankrupt and died. Then this lawyer some years after fell back upon Mama to make her pay for what he lost by neglecting to collect and the interest brought it up to several thousand. All our friends are indignant at the way we have been treated. Last summer he had the house put up for sale at a time when property was greatly depreciated and hardly anyone about here at these depressed times have any money and the house just sold for four thousand dollars - which he says does not cover his debt and he has levied an execution on our property which is the furniture &c to pay five hundred dollars. He has not issued the execution but has a decree of the Court to that effect - so any day we may expect. We have some fine valuables left - some handsome silver, china and one or two fine furnishings. One of the latter is a superb portrait of Gen. Washington painted by the celebrated Gilbert Stuart whom you know was the great artist in the days of the revolution; it is life sized - what they call kit kat (three quarters) it would be splendid for an public hall or any where; everyone who sees it pronounces it very fine. My step father Col Tuley purchased it in New York in 1825 so it been in the family for sixty years - he was in new York and attended the sale of pictures belonging to some rich man who failed in business and these paintings were sold. Now dear George I will tell you why I am troubling you with our woes and distress. We are so anxious to raise part of the money at least to pay off this five thousand and I thought if you would be so very kind as to interest yourself on our behalf and see if you could not get some one to buy it from us. They could

*get in the cars and reach Winchester in two or three hours to see the picture.
We are so pressed for money we would take three hundred or two hundred fifty.
I thought it is worth a thousand. Stuarts pictures of Washington are so scarce
and valuable. I shall feel very grateful to you. As for the present we are without
a home or shall be in a short time we expect to go to Tuleyries our lovely old
home and spend the winter with Mrs. Boyce who owns the place she was a niece
of my step father's and her husband bought the property. She has been very
kind and most affectionate and pressing for us to come to her. Our means are
so limited we are not able even to rent a house. Mama has some means but the
difficulty is to collect. She has been cheated by fraud and false hood out of a
large fortune and the losses caused by the war. It is sad and almost breaks my
heart to see her in her old age deprived of nearly everything. Everybody who
owed her took advantage of her. ... All his dreadful trouble has come upon us
like a thunderball, and often I wonder if it is really me I brought up with every
luxury and had nearly everything I wanted, to be reduced to it seems more than
I can bear at times.*

It is quite a remarkable letter. That Mary Tuley, after twenty-five years of struggling with the shattered economy of the region and the legal system, was reduced to such a situation is as unbelievable as her daughter suggests. The ultimate irony is the fact that she was forced to consider the hospitality of Belinda and Upton Boyce who, having forced her to make two trips to St. Louis to hire counsel to collect debts owed by Sarah Wright to Colonel Tuley's estate when all interested parties were in Virginia, had contributed to her downfall. It is not known if she went to The Tuleyries or where she was living when she died in 1891. She was buried at the Old Chapel Cemetery as was her daughter in 1905.

Despite the bankruptcy of the Shenandoah Valley Railroad, the Boyces continued to live in a manner which Colonel Tuley would have appreciated. *The Staunton Spectator* referred to Boyce as having a "wide reputation as an intelligent farmer and breeder" in an 1883 article reporting that he offered a premium at the Agricultural Fair in Winchester for the Shorthorn herd excelling his own. His sons, Lawrence and Truxton, advertised that the thoroughbred *Blast*, son of the first Kentucky Derby winner *Aristides*, would stand at stud at The Tuleyries in 1893. Brown in the *Annals* relays that the Boyces would entertain "almost everyone" in Clarke County once or twice a year. He also quotes a report of a gathering in 1896 that,

*... for a week past ... the beautiful home of Colonel and Mrs. U. L. Boyce has
been in possession of a house party, composed of merry young people of the
neighborhood, and on Friday night, as a fitting close to the gayeties of the
week, a German was given by the genial host and his charming wife, to which
were invited the elite of the county.... . The house and grounds were beautifully
decorated for the occasion, and the music, rendered by a well-trained orchestra,
was delightfully inspiring. ... Refreshments were served in the intermissions,
and the dawn was almost breaking when the dancers left for their homes.*

At another party in 1898, the "mansion and grounds, [were] bathed in the radiance of

Colonel Upton Lawrence Boyce

Belinda Frances Wright Boyce

a full moon, brilliantly lighted from garret to cellar, and decorated with the choicest flowers of greenhouse and garden."

The Colonel remained interested in various businesses. In October 1898 he sold a tract of mineral land in Colorado for $125,000. In 1901, he was the organizer for a group promoting a bank in Boyce. He received a patent for a device to consume smoke from furnaces. In 1899, he demonstrated it at the Treasury Department in Washington and it was declared a success. However, his efforts proved financially draining and the end was drawing near. John Wayland relays in his *Historic Homes of Northern Virginia* that,

> *In their declining years, and after prosperity had departed, Colonel and Mrs. Boyce still welcomed their friends to 'Tuleyries' and spared not their limited resources in trying to make them comfortable. Occasionally they would make a trip to Winchester, in the sadly worn panoply of former days. An ancient Negro coachman, in livery that once was new; silver mounted harness that was tied together here and there with strings; an old gentleman with courtly mien and manners; an old lady, gracious and winsome in faded finery … .*

Belinda Boyce died in 1902 and the Colonel had had a stroke sometime before that. Like her uncle before her, Belinda left no will. At that point, the estate consisted of 688 acres and passed to her three sons and the son of her daughter Katherine Jones. A 210-acre portion was deeded to her grandson, then a minor, in 1902. The mansion house and 206 acres were sold to Graham F. Blandy by deed dated September 1, 1903, for $20,000. 185 acres of the estate were originally sold to other parties and were purchased by Blandy for $11,000 on November 4, 1904. On December 4, 1904, Uriel Boyce and his daughters sold their 86 acres to Blandy for $6,000. On February 7, 1905, Blandy purchased the 210 acres allotted to U. L. Jones for $10,500, thereby reassembling the property as Colonel Boyce had done before him. The Colonel and his three sons moved to Delaware where they ran a dairy farm and a farm implement business. Colonel Boyce died in Delaware on Christmas Eve, 1907. His body was returned to the Old Chapel Cemetery where his wife and daughter were buried. Thus ended the Tuley connection to The Tuleyries.

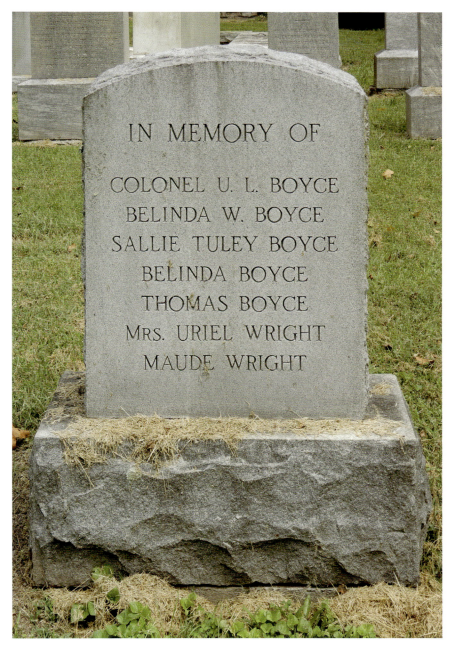

IN MEMORY OF

COLONEL U. L. BOYCE
BELINDA W. BOYCE
SALLIE TULEY BOYCE
BELINDA BOYCE
THOMAS BOYCE
Mrs. URIEL WRIGHT
MAUDE WRIGHT

Boyce and Wright family marker at the Old Chapel Cemetery,
Boyce, Virginia

Georgette and Graham Blandy

THE BLANDYS

Who was Graham Blandy and what prompted him to buy The Tuleyries?

To take up the first question first, Graham Furber Blandy was born in New York on December 17, 1868 to Graham Blandy and Emmeline H. Cruse Blandy who had moved to New York in 1863 from Philadelphia. The senior Graham was a member of the Stock Exchange from 1878 until his death in 1890 and sat on the Gold Exchange. While Emmeline was from New York, her husband was born in Newark, Delaware, and the family maintained connections to the area. They had one other son, Isaac Cruse Blandy, who had sons Graham Furber the second and third, just to keep matters interesting. They were all part of the Blandy family of wine fame still thriving on the island of Madeira. The family was originally from Dorset and, as the story goes, the first Graham's uncle, John Davis Blandy, served in Madeira during the Napoleonic wars and returned to the island with his brothers Thomas and George in 1811. John stayed and founded the wine business which continues to this day. Thomas came to America and George went to Brazil. The brothers' father is said to have been Charles and his father's name is unknown although a picture of him marked "my great great grandfather Blandy" survives at The Tuleyries. The American and Madeira branches of the family remained in contact throughout the younger Graham's life and he left a small bequest to his cousin and godchild, Percy Graham Blandy of Funchal, Madeira, in his will.

An entry in the 1924 *Who's Who in New York* states that Graham Furber Blandy was educated in New York, France, Switzerland, and was an 1885 graduate of the Germantown Academy outside Philadelphia. What he did and where he did it in France and Switzerland are not recorded. As a young man in New York, he was from all indications a well-liked man about town, and in photographs he often has a somewhat impish look. In his twenties and early thirties, his name regularly appeared in the Brooklyn papers. In 1896, he was helping organize a "music ride" for the Cycle Club and helping organize the Brooklyn Skating Club. He served as treasurer and member of the board of governors of the Dyker Meadow Golf Club in Brooklyn in 1898. In 1899, he was noted as a member of the Crescent Athletic Club. That year also saw him on a tour of the Orient. He served on the School Board of the Borough of Brooklyn from 1900 to 1901 when he resigned the position, having moved to

Manhattan. *Who's Who* also noted that he was a member of the Union League and the Sons of the Revolution.

Like many young men of the time, Teddy Roosevelt included, Graham Blandy seems to have been attracted to the last days of the American West. An oil of him on a bucking horse by Frederic Remington, now in the collection of the R. W. Norton Art Gallery in Shreveport, Louisiana, was among several works by that artist he owned. The painting, alternatively known as *Blandy* or *The Greenhorn*, is given the date of 1900, when Remington was spending as much time in New York as the West. Where it was painted and whether the two men knew each other in New York or in the West is unknown.

Blandy is variously reported to have been a nephew of Mrs. Andrew Carnegie and Mrs. Tom Carnegie and to have been an "intimate friend" of Andrew Carnegie himself. He is also reported to

Blandy's "great great grandfather Blandy"

Blandy or *The Greenhorn*
Frederic Remington, 1900,
courtesy of the R. W. Norton Art Gallery

have been entertained at Carnegie's Scottish castle, Skibo, "several times." Two of these visits made the Brooklyn papers. In 1897, he had the "pleasure of golfing and shooting" with Rudyard Kipling and in the fall of 1899, he was golfing at St. Andrews when his iron shot killed an unsuspecting squirrel. All of that notwithstanding, the actual connection is hard to pin down. Andrew and Tom had no other siblings. Blandy's mother's maiden name was Cruse and Andrew Carnegie's wife, Louise, was the daughter of John William Whitfield and Fannie Miner Davis Whitfield. Besides Louise, they had three children, one of whom died in infancy, a daughter who never married, and a son. Thomas's wife was Lucy Ackerman Coleman Carnegie, the daughter of William and Nancy Trovillo Coleman. She was one of six children but of her three sisters who married, none became a Blandy. The connection must have gone back at least one more generation but it continued throughout Blandy's life as Louise Carnegie visited The Tuleyries in the fall of 1922.

As with so many things a century on, the specific nature of Blandy's work as a broker is unknown. However, like Colonel Boyce before him, he was involved in various railroads. In 1895, he recovered a judgment for indebtedness incurred by one William H. Howell who speculated in railroad stocks in 1881. In 1900, he bought 600 shares of the New York & Harlem Railroad Co. at what was purported to be the highest price paid for the stock to that date. In 1903, he and his brother Isaac were among the directors of the Greenwich & Johnsonville Railway Co. when it merged with the Battenkill Railroad to meet the competition of the Northern New York trolley. He was a vice president of the Railway in 1907 and his brother served as its president. He entertained George Gould, president of the Wabash Railroad and son of the legendary railroad man Jay Gould, at The Tuleyries in 1905. At about the same time, he was a plaintiff in litigation against the New York & Harlem Railroad Co. in which William K. and Frederick W. Vanderbilt were defendants. He was reported in 1909 to own 1,000 shares of the Delaware & Hudson Company, one of the country's oldest and longest-surviving railroads which began as a canal company. The suit involving the Vanderbilts dragged on until at least 1912 when he was part of a committee seeking to obtain more than the $175 which had been offered for $50 shares of that railroad. That year, he was listed as one of the twelve largest shareholders of the New York Central Railroad although his 1,000 shares paled by comparison to the 30,000-share controlling interest of Charles Pratt & Co. In 1911, he reacquired a seat on the New York Stock Exchange, which he held for the rest of his life.

Whether railroads were his primary interest or a sideline, by the time he decided to get married and his engagement was announced in November 1907, he was described as "extremely well known in business circles and in society." *The New York Times* also reported that, "Some years ago he made quite a fortune in being a member of the New York Stock Exchange, and retiring for a while he spent several years in European travel." This seems to have occurred prior to his move to Manhattan in 1901. When he left Brooklyn, he purchased a home at 26 East 38th Street. He and his mother traveled to Europe prior to the move to purchase pictures and furniture for the new house. He also hit the auction houses, purchasing a painting by German artist Adolf Schreyer entitled "Arabs Crossing a Stream." The auction was of the collection of F. O. Matthiessen, a founder of the Sugar Trust, and the star of the show was a Rubens "Holy Family." Blandy paid the same price, $13,000, for his painting as was paid at the auction for a Titian of the Doge Grimani. A Rembrandt sold for $16,000. He was apparently a more astute financier than art collector.

What prompted Graham Blandy to purchase The Tuleyries? About the only anwers that come to mind after considerable research are the classics: because he could and because everyone else was doing it. He clearly had the means and in the early 1900s many wealthy northerners were caught up in the rage for country houses and hunting properties all along the East Coast. The increased congestion of large cities and the ease of rail transportation led many past the immediate vicinity of New York to Virginia and, for those who particularly enjoyed shooting, to the decrepit plantations of coastal South Carolina and the Red Clay region of Georgia. Although he apparently enjoyed shooting at Skibo - for years many trophies of those days hung at The Tuleyries - this does not seem to have been his passion. It was agriculture that caught his attention, possibly inspired by the farming activities of his friends, the Carnegies, on Cumberland Island, and The Tuleyries was quite a farm.

To help him turn his dream into brick and mortar, Blandy turned to Philadelphia architect Mantle Fielding. The two had overlapped at the Germantown Academy, Fielding graduating in 1883 and Blandy in 1885. Fielding went on to study at MIT and by 1886 was back in Philadelphia where his work concentrated on residential commissions, often of stone and in a Colonial Revival version of the Pennsylvania farm house. His lasting fame is not from his architectural work but from his authorship of the *Dictionary of American Painters, Sculptors, and Engravers* which was published in 1926 and remains a respected authority on the subject.

 Blandy had agreed to allow the Boyces to remain in residence until the Colonel could make the move to Delaware. This was accomplished sometime in 1904 and by January 1905, Fielding had forwarded blueprints for renovations to the mansion house. In an accompanying letter, he wrote, "You noticed that I have endeavored to carry out the new work exactly in the same lines as the old, and that I have also kept it as simple as possible, although I have provided for work being done in a substantial and lasting manner."

The most visible part of his work involved enclosing the conservatory and cellar below. On the interior, the most extensive work was the installation of three bathrooms on the second floor. Dealing with a problem which has existed ever since plumbing came indoors to houses not designed to accommodate it, Fielding had to figure out where to put these new necessities. His answer was to insert one between the two bedrooms on the northeast side of the house, straddling the archway the Boyces inserted when they removed the wall between the two rooms below to create their dining or ballroom. To further weaken things at that point, a window was inserted where the wall he removed had joined the exterior wall. On the opposite side of the house, a bath was inserted adjacent to the wall above the massive double doors which separated the twin parlors. The third was installed above the pantry at the rear of the house. Building atop the two voids was problematic enough but rather than try to channel plumbing through twelve and sixteen-inch solid brick walls, the pipes were laid over the second-story floors and encased in concrete. New floors were then installed above that. For the next 75 years, this produced a visibly seamless answer to the age-old problem.

After a few more minor improvements, Blandy and Fielding moved to the farm buildings. The smokehouse, Garden House or seed house, and the Porter Lodge or main gate are mentioned in the 1845 article about The Tuleyries quoted earlier. The foundry or well house, gas house or carriage house, and the stable are believed to have been built during the Tuleys' tenure as well. Given the different names given to different buildings at different times, it is difficult to determine exactly who did what to which in what order. It appears that Blandy and Fielding first turned their attention to the garage which had served as the gas house prior to Blandy's purchase of the property. After the Boyces installed gas lighting in the mansion, equipment to provide the gas for it from coal was housed in this building. It was converted into a carriage house at the time renovations to the house were being completed and in recent times has been called the garage although it now serves as a workshop. Next to get attention was the stable. By August, 1905, Fielding had prepared blueprints for renovating the building. Instructions to the contractor stated that it was to be repaired and rebuilt in the same manner as the old gas house.

This brings up the question of the Dutch or stepped gables. In an extensive assessment of the buildings at The Tuleyries completed in 1989, John Milner Associates, the highly respected architecture and preservation firm from West Chester, Pennsylvania, stated that, "It cannot be confirmed at present that the stepped gables at the Chicken House, or at any of the early outbuildings existed prior to 1905. While we believe that they did exist, … [a]ll of the stepped gables with the possible exception of those of the Foundry, are constructed of 1905 brickwork." While it has been suggested that the Tuleys picked up the idea for the motif while traveling in the Netherlands, there is no evidence that either ever went farther than Cuba. The idea may have come from the Porter Lodge, or if the Barracks preceded the construction of the house, it may have been the origin of stepped gables at The Tuleyries, or it may simply have been the fashion in Clarke County as shown by the dependencies added at Smithfield in 1847 and the facade of the neighboring Wickliffe Church built in 1846.

Smithfield dependency

Wickliffe Church

Comparison between the gable ends of the gas house, the forge, and the stable as rebuilt in 1905 shows that the foundry or forge rather than the gas house was the model for rebuilding the stepped gables which survive today on the service buildings. The gables at the forge are set on corbelled string courses but otherwise have flat surfaces while the gable ends of the gas house are distinguished by pilasters which rise unbroken to the top of the first two steps.

Perhaps the oldest of the outbuildings and another which was repaired and rebuilt in this first round of rehabilitation is the chicken house or dairy as it was later called. Its gables were clearly copied from those of the forge, including the two diamond-shaped vents in each gable. It is the only one of the brick buildings on the farm constructed on a stone foundation although the smokehouse is entirely constructed of stone.

While Blandy and Fielding were having fun at the farm, one Georgette Haven Borland was making her debut in New York. Georgette was born on February 11, 1886 to John Nelson and Alice Griswold Haven Borland. They presented her to New York society at back-to-back receptions on Friday and Saturday, December 9 and 10, 1904, at their home at 116 East 37th Street, a block south across Park Avenue from Blandy's home at 26 East 38th. A descendant of several distinguished New England families, her father sat on the

Gable end of the chicken house or dairy

Chicken house or dairy

Gable end of the forge or well house

Forge or well house

New York Stock Exchange with Blandy. Her paternal grandfather, Dr. John Nelson Borland, was a Boston physician. Her maternal grandfather was George Griswold Haven, a New York banker who served as president of the Metropolitan Opera and Real Estate Company and was one of the 98 men listed in 1908 by Progressive Senator Robert LaFollette as controlling "all the financial, industrial, and commercial business of the country." While it would not have been of as much concern to the senator from Wisconsin, Haven was also the gentleman who decided who got which box at the opera.

Miss Borland was a graduate of the Brearley School in Manhattan, a highly regarded girls' preparatory school, and may have attended Bard College. When and how she met Graham Blandy is unknown but it could have been on the street in the neighborhood, at Tuxedo Park, at the opera, or at any one of the many places where New York's elite society crossed paths. Georgette was clearly a part of the city's social elite She was among the 350 guests invited to the costume ball hosted by James Hazen Hyde at Sherry's Hotel on January 31, 1905. The hotel was converted into a flowered scene from 18th-century France and the party was from all reports considered a grand success until reactions to its extravagance and corporate opportunism forced Hyde to relinquish control of his father's company, Equitable Life Assurance Society, and head for self-imposed exile in France. If Graham Blandy was

Gable end of stable

Stable

Gable end of gas house

Gas house, carriage house, or garage

Alice (Elsie), Madeline (Baby), and Georgette Borland, early 1890s

there, he was one of the few attendees who avoided having their photograph taken and his costume preserved for posterity.

Even if they did not meet at the ball, they surely crossed paths in the fall of that year as Graham and Georgette, her parents, and her sisters, were all first-class passengers on the *St. Louis* which sailed from Southampton, England, to New York. In any novel worth its price in paperback, Graham would have booked passage to have the opportunity to woo Georgette. For all we now know, they ended up on the same ship making an Atlantic crossing by sheer coincidence. However it happened, they apparently took a liking to each other

Georgette Borland and two other guests at the James Hazen Hyde Ball, January 31, 1905

Georgette Haven Borland Blandy Bull by Francis Day (1863-1942), *courtesy of Ocean's Bridge*

Graham Furber Blandy, *courtesy of the Blandy Experimental Farm and Thomas Flory*

despite the eighteen-year age gap which was noted in the newspapers. Their engagement was announced in *The New York Times* on October 11, 1907 and the wedding was set for January 30, 1908, at the Church of the Incarnation at 35th and Madison Avenue near their homes. *The Times* later noted that the event was to be "among the smart weddings" of the month.

The wedding did not occur as announced. Two different stories appeared in the newspapers and there is some hint that Georgette may have gotten cold feet. In early January the Brooklyn papers reported that the wedding had been postponed due to the illness of the bride. The wedding finally occurred on April 29, 1908, at the Borland home before close family with Isaac Blandy, his brother's best man, as the only attendant. The ceremony was performed by the Rev. William Fitz-Simon of St. Mary's Church in Tuxedo Park. Reports of the wedding in the Manhattan papers attributed the cause of the delay to the illness and March 18 death of Georgette's grandfather Haven.

The couple took up residence at Blandy's home on 38th Street and presumably spent their first summer together at The Tuleyries. The next summer, they sailed on the *Lusitania* for Europe on July 28, returning in mid-October. They were accompanied by Georgette's parents and sisters. Sister Elsie recorded in her trip diary that after an initial time in England, the group progressed to Scotland where Georgette and Graham parted company from the rest of the Borlands to visit the Carnegies at Skibo while the others toured Stirling Castle. Then it was on to Paris.

By the following summer, they were engaged in a number of projects at The Tuleyries. In February 1910, contractor James L. Gardner presented an estimate for building a cattle barn and another in May to build a "hay barracks." In March, he proposed to complete the carriage house. This latter building had been designed by Winchester architect Stuart H. Edmonds who noted on his plans that, "In general this bldg. is to match the stable." The most interesting thing about the carriage house as built is that a slate flashing course was installed at ground level and at the top of the walls in an attempt to control the moisture which had caused so much damage to the older outbuildings. Edmonds' drawing also shows flared walls which narrowed as they rose above the foundations, possibly another effort to shed water from the foundations. This detail was not followed although, being a newer building and wholly constructed of factory brick, it has survived in better condition than any of the other brick outbuildings. There is no indication why Blandy turned to Edmonds rather than to his friend Fielding for this building. It may have been that it, being a copy of Fielding's prior work, could be assigned to a local practitioner or it may have been that Fielding was busy with other things at the time.

The cattle barn and the hay barracks were needed to house Blandy's Herefords. He seems to have begun the cattle business in earnest by purchasing the herd of a neighbor, Charles E. Clapp of Rosemont Farm near Berryville, in March 1906. Clapp's 70 Herefords included the prominent bull Acrobat and reportedly cost Blandy $8,000. Although the article reporting the sale said Blandy's entry into the business was a "diversion," he took it very seriously for some time. By 1911, the herd was apparently at its prime, winning eight ribbons at the state fair in Richmond - none were blue - and his principal competitor was one W. S. Van Netta who had been in the business since at least the 1890s. A major sale was held at The Tuleyries in June 1910 and another in 1913. There must have been more sales as at least seventeen copper photogravure plates of various cattle survive at the farm today.

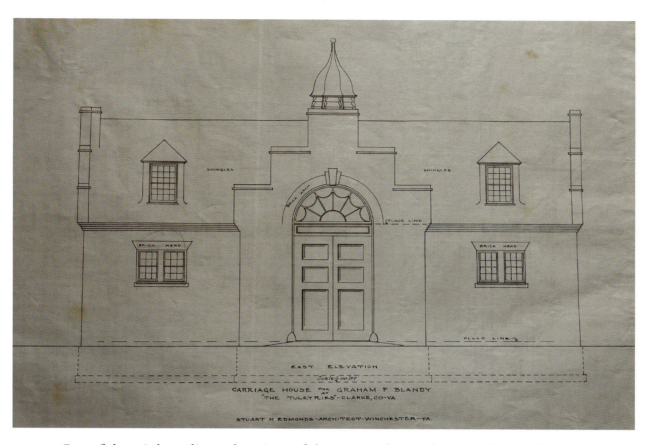

One of three ink-on-linen elevations of the carriage house drawn by Stuart Edmonds in 1910

Preparations underway in 1910 for construction of Edmonds' carriage house

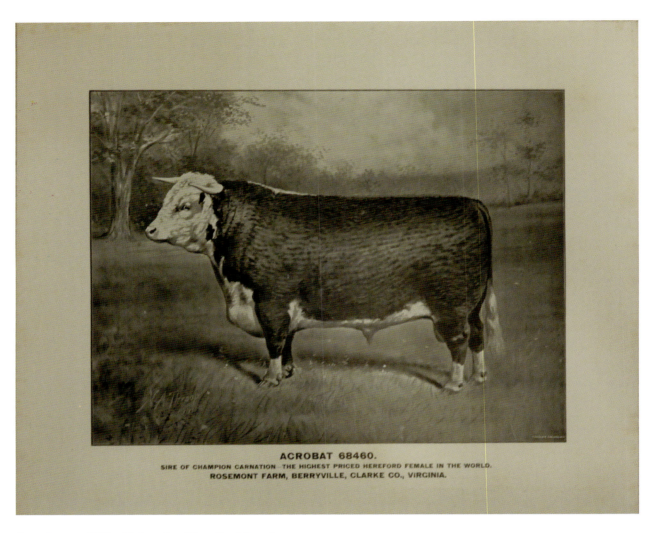

ACROBAT 68460.

SIRE OF CHAMPION CARNATION—THE HIGHEST PRICED HEREFORD FEMALE IN THE WORLD.

ROSEMONT FARM, BERRYVILLE, CLARKE CO., VIRGINIA.

Acrobat and The Tuleyries Hereford herd

An extensive article ran in the August 1916 issue of *The Field Illustrated* entitled "The Return of the Hereford." This was not a magazine focused on people who were making a living from the soil but on people of wealth who found agricultural pursuits an appropriate leisure activity or "diversion" on their country estates. The list of the magazine's founding members included an Astor, a du Pont, and a Vanderbilt. While the bulk of the 1916 article focused on herds in New England, all its illustrations came from The Tuleyries. The article tells that the herd was begun in 1903 with the purchase of 25 heifers and augmented with the purchase of a herd of 66 head in 1904. As there is no record of Blandy purchasing a second herd, it is assumed that the article refers to the purchase from Charles Clapp. At the time of the article, the herd consisted of 85 head of "choice stock." Blandy was quoted in the article explaining his approach to the herd.

> *I have never asked excessive prices for calves and prefer the steady sales to farmers at prices they can pay to the speculator ones sometimes obtained by large breeders who devote much pains and expense to fitting animals for show purposes with extra nurse cows.*
>
> *I try to produce sires which will carry on the best traditions of the breed for regular farm herds, where the farmer wants the sire to produce beef for the market. On one island off the coast of Georgia, where for years my bulls have gone, the entire herd of common grade cattle has been transformed into a herd of about 300 almost pure bred heifers, weighing at the same age, twice what they did formerly. This has been accomplished solely by the use of pure bred bulls at an expenditure by the owner of the island of less than $1,000.*

One strongly suspects that the island off the coast of Georgia was Cumberland Island, owned by and home of his friend, Lucy Coleman Carnegie. The article notes that in 1914 Blandy shipped cattle to Uruguay, which became the foundation for many Hereford herds in South America. The real interest of the quote is his obvious concern for his farmer neighbors. He was especially involved in the local community during 1911 and 1912, sponsoring prizes for the best corn crop in Clarke County and holding the exhibition on the lawn at The Tuleyries in the latter year. He also awarded prizes for the largest flock of turkeys. The *Richmond Times-Dispatch* reported that, "his generous attitude toward the farmers of Clarke County has resulted in much keen but friendly competition."

Blandy also became very interested in growing apples and peaches, planting hundreds of trees. Orchards were a major feature in early 20th-century attempts to diversify the local agricultural economy. Blandy went so far as to have Fielding design a dormitory or orchard lodge for workers who came to pick the crop, as well as a packing house. The lodge, attached to a preexisting building, was under construction in 1912 but is thought to have burned in 1926. The location and fate of the packing house are unknown. Maps of the estate during his tenure refer to the area south of the lawn as the "60 acre orchard."

When the crop came in, it was not a diversion but all hands on deck. In a letter dated Monday, September 27, believed to have been written in 1920, Georgette relayed farm news to her sister Elsie. "We sold all our apples on the trees but we pick + pack + haul to station getting 2.00 a barrel. We did well as apples are a glut this year. G. is busy all day at the packing house and I have helped quite a lot at the sorting + grading tables. Over 1000

Preparing peaches for shipment by train to market

The orchard lodge designed by Fielding and built in 1912

The "Anderson House" photographed in 1912

The Millwood Colored School

barrels gone already." In 1914, Blandy had figured his profit from 1,002 barrels of apples at $600.32. Peaches were also a major part of the orchard and they, as well as chickens and other produce, were regularly shipped to Georgette's mother, Mrs. Borland, and others in New York. In another letter from Georgette to her sister, Elsie, she reported that "all the men are busy baling + shipping a hundred tons of hay to Florida." Clearly the operation at The Tuleyries was more than a diversion to the Blandys.

During these years, H. L. Martin served as farm manager. He and his family lived in the two-story white frame house near the northwest boundary of the farm. It had been built by 1912 when photographs label it as "Anderson's house." Martin was responsible for hiring and managing the permanent and temporary workers necessary to run the farm and harvest the crops. When the Blandys were away from White Post, either in New York for the winter or traveling, Martin wrote weekly letters detailing the weather, progress of work on the farm, and general news in the community. He must have been both a rather crusty character and a highly loyal and trusted employee who did not want anyone messing with The Tuleyries or its crops or livestock. In December of 1922 he wrote Blandy that, "I sent [the Hunt Club] word that if they did not stay away that I would use my gun on their dogs and them too if necessary." Blandy's response does not survive but Martin's next letter leads one to believe that Blandy was more interested in cordial relations with his neighbors than the damage the fox hunters might cause.

Agriculture was not Blandy's only interest. He was very concerned with the education of the local population and black children in particular. In 1909, he gave the local board of education $4,000 which was used in 1910 to construct schools for black children in Millwood and White Post. Both of these buildings still stand although the school in White Post has been converted into a residence. The building in Millwood remains virtually unaltered since its construction and was listed on the National Register of Historic Places in 2000. Intended to operate as a manual training or industrial school, the one-story, two-room building served as an elementary school until 1952 and has been a community center since that time.

Georgette also became involved with the local community. She served as the secretary-treasurer of the Millwood Improvement Association in 1911. Its stated goal was to ensure that Millwood was "kept clean and attractive at all times." Her fellow officers were Mrs. Hugh Nelson of Long Branch and Mrs. Henry B. Gilpin. However, Georgette's primary country interests were her garden and her dogs. She developed extensive gardens to the northwest of the house between the smokehouse and the garden house. She began planning the garden in 1908 and it evolved over time as seen in sketches from her garden book. The borders of her flower and vegetable beds were outlined in box which survive today, grown so large that they obscure the original design. She loved roses and cutting them to bring into the house. There were rows of lilies, climbing roses, and more boxwoods. Careful planting lists were made each year. An arched gate referencing the entry was added to plans by Stuart Edmonds. Sculptures, and a summer house smothered in a climbing rose enhanced the scene. As for the dogs, Georgette was often photographed with one of her pet Pekingese who had a special bed on the front porch of the house where they and guests often relaxed to enjoy the evening light over the Blue Ridge.

Georgette seems to have had some ideas about the house as well. Contractor Gardner submitted a bill for adding a window to the library in May of 1912. Heaping guess upon conjecture, one suspects that this is the rear window of the room and that its addition was

Georgette on the rear steps of The Tuleyries with the bounty from her garden

Georgette's garden in its prime in 1924

necessitated by the enclosure of the conservatory. The doorway to the rooms in the former conservatory had likely been a window and when the conservatory space was no longer lit by a full wall of windows, the library would have been much darker.

A new gateway to the south was also added to the walls surrounding the house. Designed by Stuart Edmonds to complement the Porter Lodge, it is believed to have been built after 1910. He may also have been responsible for the final building which formed the quadrangle composed of the stable, dairy, and coach house. This stucco building, the only one on the property, features the same stepped gables above a corbelled string course as the other buildings. It was designed to have four stalls, a tack room, and the only indoor toilet in the quadrangle but does not appear to have been built with horses in mind. At some point, likely after construction of this building, all of the outbuildings were painted white and must have presented a site reminiscent of stable blocks and service courts the Blandys had seen in Europe. Why the stucco building was not aligned with the dairy it faces is one of those questions which lingers.

Graham and Georgette appear to have settled into a pleasant routine of spending their winters in New York and summers in Virginia. World War I does not seem to have interfered with that pattern to any great extent. Graham served on a committee of brokers and bankers who sought to relieve some of the stress caused their employees by the closure of the New York Stock Exchange from August through November, 1914. This closure was precipitated by American fears that as the European powers went to war against each other, they would seek to sell their American assets to fund the conflict, causing a run on the market and the banks. After the United States entered the war, Graham's nephew and namesake served in a medical unit in France, a fact which may have prompted him to lead Stock Exchange efforts to fund motorized ambulances for the American Field Service there. Fears that the war would reach American shores must have been real at the time. Georgette was part of a group of Manhattan women who raised funds to support an "auto field dressing station" which could be moved around the city if needed. Graham led a group from Wall Street who petitioned the Red Cross to establish a "Stock Exchange Branch" to aid in its work in 1917 and served for some time as an assistant director of the organization in Washington.

America's entry into the war did not bring everything to a halt. New York society continued to gather and the newspapers continued to write about it. Georgette and Graham were part of the scene, attending the wedding of J. P. Morgan's daughter on Long Island in July, 1917. A letter reported, "Last night we dined with the Baruchs - quite a party." They also considered more building at The Tuleyries and again sought out Mantle Fielding. In October, 1917, the architect presented plans for adding a second floor and porches to the gas house to convert it into a servants' dormitory. A letter of 1917 also refers to designs for a tenant house. 1922 saw the arrival of electricity to the main house. While Blandy had contracted with the local power company to run lines to the farm in 1920, the visit of Louise Carnegie two years later may have prompted him to bring the main house into the 20th century.

There were bumps in the road. Around 1921, Mrs. Borland wrote her daughter Elsie that Graham had a leaking heart valve and that Mr. Borland believed Graham's finances were "low." Blandy had sold a major portion of the Hereford herd to a gentleman in Indiana in late 1919. Sometime around 1920 - the Borlands and their daughters were prolific letter writers but rarely included the year in the date of their missives - Georgette was laid up with an eye disease and was again forced to bed for over a month in 1926 with "sleeping sickness" and may also have suffered from colitis. By 1925, Blandy was seeking to reduce his farming activity. H. L. Martin - who dated his letters - responded to him on the matter:

> *I believe the orchard alone + rent grass is your idea of handling the farm and to get rid of work + worry etc. but a place like this kept up right without some work or worry on the part of some one is an impossibility and the thing for you to do is to find the way you want it done that it will give you the most satisfaction and least worry + let someone do it + you not worry and get your mind on better things.*

While he may have been cutting back at the farm, Blandy was still willing to take on a project. In 1925, he took up the cause of what was then believed to have been George Washington's office when he worked as a surveyor for Lord Fairfax between 1749 and 1751. He carried on extensive correspondence with Mrs. Nellie C. Kennerly who owned the property which had been Fairfax's home, Greenway Court. He sought to raise money for the project in both Virginia and New York for restoration of the small, one-story stone building. He also corresponded with Albert, 12th Lord Fairfax of Cameron in London. Fairfax replied that if the building had been the Proprietary Office, it could not have been built until 1761. This seems to have slowed the project but those never wanting facts to interfere with a good story repeat the legend of Washington's connection to the building down to the present day.

Graham Blandy did not survive to see the project completed. Sometime in the winter of 1926, he contracted pneumonia and after what his obituary described as a six-weeks' illness, part of which was spent at Johns Hopkins, he died at his home in New York on March 25, 1926. His funeral service was conducted at the Church of the Incarnation where he and Georgette had first planned to be married. He was buried near his parents at the cemetery surrounding the ancient St. James' Mill Creek Episcopal Church in what is now suburban Wilmington, Delaware.

The Fairfax Proprietary Office restored in 1930 and again in 2009

Ginkgo grove at the Blandy Experimental Farm/Virginia State Arboretum

THE **B** ULLS

Graham Blandy's death in 1926 followed an extended illness and was therefore not completely unexpected. On the other hand, a major term of his will seems to have caught both Georgette and the University of Virginia by surprise. In a document dated November 5, 1925, he left $500 each to his farm manager, H. L. Martin, and his cousin from Madeira, and substantial bequests to his brother Isaac and his nephews, Graham, Alexander, and Dallam. He left the contents of the Manhattan house to Georgette and requested that she leave his paintings to the Metropolitan Museum of Art at her death. He left the mansion house at The Tuleyries and 210 acres which included all the outbuildings northwest of the house to Georgette as well as stock in the New York & Harlem Railroad Company and the income from the remainder of his estate for her life.

The kicker was item 9. In it, Blandy left 700 acres of The Tuleyries, including the slave quarters and other buildings to the southeast of the Porter Lodge to the University of Virginia provided that it agreed to call the property "The Blandy Experimental Farm and [to] run it to teach boys farming in the various branches, including fruit raising." After Georgette's death, his will provided for additional bequests to his brother and nephews but the remainder of his estate was directed to UVA if it had accepted the farm.

White Post being some two hours north of Charlottesville and UVA having no existing agricultural program, there was considerable question whether the university would accept the gift. There were also questions about how roads and utility lines which served the portion of the farm left to Georgette but ran through the property left to the university would be treated. These issues prompted Georgette to bring suit naming the Rector and Visitors of the University of Virginia seeking clarification. The action was filed in Clarke Circuit Court in July 1926. Considerable paper was expended on the question of whether the land would pass under the will's residuary clause or go directly to Blandy's brother Isaac if UVA did not accept the gift. However, the university decided that the bequest was too good to pass up even if inconveniently located and that issue was never reached. An order was entered by the court on December 9, 1927 addressing the utility and access issues and on October 13, 1928, the court found that UVA had complied with the will and that it had created "a charitable trust to be forever operated, maintained, and conducted" by the university and the case was closed.

Lacking an agricultural program, UVA hired Orland Emile White, a geneticist, as Professor of Agricultural Biology and Director of the Blandy Experimental Farm in 1927. The program which White developed bore little if any relation to the language of Blandy's will which envisioned a curriculum which would "teach boys farming in the various branches." What White created was a program where up to five graduate students lived at the farm for the summer and one of the university's three annual terms and pursued research into plant genetics. To accommodate the program, White set about converting The Tuleyries' slave quarters into housing for himself and the students. While the living conditions verged on the primitive, White was taken with the surrounding landscape which he described in a letter to his wife.

> *The peaches are in bloom & shortly the apples will be. Pear orchards & sweet cherries have been in bloom for some time and in the bare spots in the orchard and on blue grass stretches, millions of johnny jump up - little blue, forget-me-not like violets are in bloom. It's a lovely country. Banks of yellow and blue violets fill the forest and along the roadsides. Between the trees of weeping willow, boxelder and paper mulberry, the view is superb - stretching away to the Shennandoah river and the mountains. Sheep graze in the near distance on our velvet green pastures & bees ceaselessly hum in the cherry trees. Altogether it's a beautiful pastoral scene.*

In addition to the genetic research, White set about gathering and planting all manner of flowers, shrubs, and trees on the property, at one point saying, "We are going to try to make the blooming place like a blooming English garden." The effort was not just for aesthetics. It was primarily designed to see what plants would thrive in the local climate. Varieties of orange were planted as well as such things as palmetto palm and dwarf pomegranates. Ultimately, some 6,000 different species of plants were assembled at Blandy. One of the most striking features of the farm created by White was the ginkgo grove. Ginkgoes being both male and female, the grove grew out of White's study of the sex ratio of their seeds. One of the new students collected seeds each fall from a tree on the university campus.

> *On a fine sunny, Saturday afternoon in fall, when everyone else went to the football game, this poor fellow would have to pick up these fruits. He would about fill a metal waste basket and bring it to Dr. White's office. New Ginkgo fruit smells a little like a room that a cat has been in for a long time. Dr. White would leave them sit there for weeks, until it got so bad that practically the whole building smelled of them. Then he would plant the seeds and, when the trees were big enough, he and the fellows would plant them in his Ginkgo forest.*

On a shoestring budget and far removed from the heart of the university, White, from all accounts both brilliant and eccentric, managed to establish a widely known and highly respected program for genetic research at Blandy. A byproduct was the creation of a collection of plants of all sorts which ultimately led to the designation of the farm as the Orland E. White Arboretum when he retired from the university in 1955.

The loss of her husband had predictable effects on Georgette Blandy. On September 15, 1927, her father wrote to her sister Elsie, "Your mother is pretty well but greatly worried over Georgette who seems very sad she has not been overwell. ... Personally and please keep this to yourself she is a terrible wet blanket." About the same time, Mrs. Borland wrote to Elsie of Georgette:

> She is at this time defiant, etc. If you consider the contributing causes to the condition you will be as lenient as I am Were she not nervous + desperate I would give no further advice. She has never confided in me in any way, but I fear a deep interest in Kinkalen Martin You must never say I wrote this but Georgette is far from fit to travel alone so far. She forgets, sleeps, is impatient + not a bit as she was before Graham died + she had sleeping sickness + colitis too is always nagging and making her nerves jagged -

These snippets of correspondence require several digressions to reveal their full import. In the first instance, it seems that everyone in the Borland family, mother, father, and both sisters, treated Elsie as their confidante and wrote to her religiously. This fact is likely attributable not only to her personality but also to her physical location. After receiving the name Alice, Georgette's younger sister was ever after known as Elsie. Her path in New York was similar to Georgette's and after completing Brearley and making her debut, she married Marshall Orme Wilson Jr. at the Church of the Incarnation on June 8, 1910.

The groom was the son of Marshall Orme Wilson Sr. and Caroline Schermerhorn Astor. The career of Marshall Orme Sr. was spent in the real estate and investment business of his father, Richard Thornton Wilson, along with his brother Richard T. (Dick) Wilson Jr. After Harvard, Marshall Orme Wilson Jr. entered the family firm. Although called M. Orme Wilson Jr. in the announcement of his wedding to Elsie Borland, he rarely used the name Marshall and, after having a son whom he named Orme Wilson Jr., became Orme Wilson Sr. although he never used the designation. He is described as shy and scholarly with an avid interest in art, architecture, and music. He also had an early interest in automobiles, serving as Secretary-Treasurer of the Motor Car Touring Society of the City of New York in 1908, an organization on whose board his uncle, Dick Wilson, also sat.

In 1914, he and Elsie built a stunning townhouse at 11 East 64th Street in Manhattan, just down the street from his parents. Built in a chaste French neoclassical style, it was the work of Trowbridge & Livingston, the firm which designed the St. Regis Hotel and whose client list included such New York names as Morgan and Phipps. As the story goes, Elsie so enjoyed the design and construction process and became so involved with it that someone at the firm was heard to say of her, "Here comes trouble." Both sides of the process thereafter referred to the firm as Trowbridge, Livingston & Trouble.

In September 1917, soon after the entry of the United States into World War I, Orme Sr. went to Washington to serve on the Committee on Supplies of the Council of National Defense which was soon absorbed by the Supply and Equipment Division of the Army's Quartermaster Corps. In the summer of 1918, he became a First Lieutenant and was assigned to the Military Intelligence Division of the General Staff until his discharge in March of 1919. It was likely this time in Washington that convinced him that he did not wish to return to the R. T. Wilson & Company and in April, 1920, he entered the Diplomatic Service.

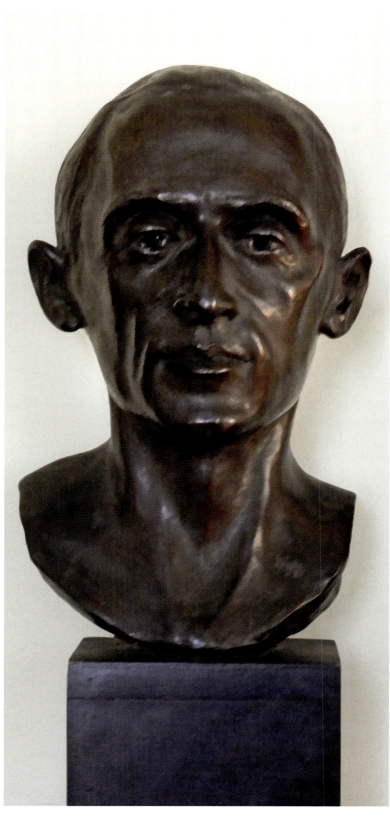

Bust of Quinquela Martin by Georgette Blandy, circa 1928

After initial postings in Brussels and Bern, he was assigned to the Embassy in Buenos Aires. Elsie and their young son accompanied him to these various postings, which explains her family's desire to keep her informed of happenings back home, and Buenos Aires brings us to "Kinkalen" Martin.

It is not remembered whether Georgette met Benito Quinquela Martin in Argentina, in New York, or in Europe. Wherever it was, he made quite an impression on her and her mother was terrified about the relationship. The third Borland sister, Madeline (sometimes called Baby), described her mother as frantic over the situation but seems to have taken it in stride, noting that her mother was "always fearful of G. and her beaux." In a letter to Elsie in Buenos Aires, Georgette described a visit to The Tuleyries where Quinquela was part of the group. "Went to Va. two weeks ago with the Coppingers and Quinquela for three days and we had a perfect time - Quinquela is a fascinating little person, so simple and yet intelligent. He sailed Saturday so you may see him before you get this as he is anxious to show you his head at once." On June 26, 1928, Georgette again wrote to her sister in Buenos Aires, "Have you seen Quinquela and the head I did of him. Am crazy to know what you think of it."

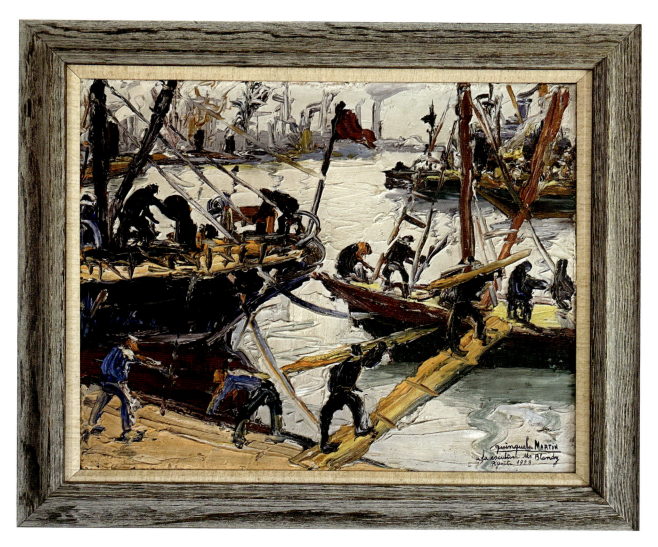

Oil on canvas by Benito Quinquela Martin, 1928, inscribed to *a la escultora. Ms Blandy Agosto 1928,*
private collection

Somewhere along the way, Georgette had taken up sculpture and it seems she began her studies at The Grand Central School of Art. Writing in late 1927, she told Elsie, "I work every morning but Saturday at my sculpture class and am enclosing some views I took myself of my first figure - the work of nine mornings. I am really quite proud of it." In the letter about the visit to Virginia, she reported that she had, "fixed up the old room in cellar of the wing as a studio and hope to continue working. Will finish Allen Mowry's head tomorrow."

By early 1929, she was not only thinking of sculpture. On February 6 of that year, she purchased what continues to be known as the Joliffe Tract, some 133 acres west of and adjacent to The Tuleyries. Seven days later, she signed a most remarkable will. The document, printed as part of later court proceedings, ran to some 25 pages and made 203 specific bequests. In its detail, it provides a virtual inventory of her prized possessions and as they say in the trade, the objects of her bounty. Among the specific bequests was $15,000 to her teacher at the School of Art, Georg Lober. The silver loving cup given to her

Three-handled loving cup given to the Blandys as a wedding present by William Coleman Carnegie and his wife, with the view of The Tuleyries shown. William's home, Stafford, and his mother's mansion, Dungeness, both on Cumberland Island, Georgia, appear on the other sides.

and Graham as a wedding present by William Coleman Carnegie, one of Lucy Carnegie's sons whom she described as Graham's "old friend", was to be returned to him. There were also bequests to Bertha and Andrew Carnegie, he being another of Lucy's sons, and to Mrs. Andrew Carnegie who is also described as "an old friend of my husband's." Mantle Fielding and the farm manager, H. J. Martin, and his family were among the many also remembered. Benito Quinquela Martin was to receive the income from $100,000 for life.

Quinquela was born in Buenos Aires in March 1890 and left at an orphanage. He was adopted by an Italian immigrant, Manuel Quinquela, whose name he later incorporated into his own. Manuel was a dock worker and ran a coal yard. His adopted son followed suit at a very young age. At 17, Benito attended drawing and painting classes and at 20, had his first exhibition of paintings. His subjects were almost exclusively the docks and dockworkers of his childhood. During the time he was connected with Georgette, he had major exhibitions in New York, Rome, Madrid, and London. In the latter city, the 1930 catalogue for the exhibition at the New Burlington Galleries featured a foreword by the director of the Tate who suggested a spiritual kinship between Martin and Van Gogh. Quinquela's home was always the La Boca section of Buenos Aires in which he spent his childhood and after returning there for good in 1931, he continued to paint and became a beloved philanthropist for the area. He did not marry until three years before his death in 1977.

It is now difficult to know whether Mrs. Borland had good reason to be frantic about the relationship between Georgette and Quinquela but even if she did, it did not last. There was clearly a serious connection between them as witnessed by the clause in the 1929 will. Perhaps it was as simple as described by Madeline in a letter to Elsie, "She said she + Kincalla lived very far apart + are very interested in each other" and absence made the heart grow yonder. Perhaps the family had been correct in pinning its "hopes on his common sense."

The relationship with Quinquela likely cooled when someone else caught Georgette's eye. While she may have known Lt. Col. Edmund Llewellyn Bull in New York, they were studying sculpture in the same studio in Paris in the spring of 1930. In a letter to Elsie written from the Savoy and dated April 18, Georgette described their courtship. "It all happened so suddenly I can hardly realize it yet, but I do know we are both very happy and are sure we are making no mistake." As sure as she was, she was still concerned about her mother's reaction. "I wish I knew how she felt about this news I surprised her with. I got her cable yesterday 'Wish you both every happiness' which was stereotypical + cold. Of course it was a shock to her and of course she does not know him so it was hard for her to feel happy about it."

In May 1930, her engagement to Lt. Col. Edmund Llewellyn Bull was announced. A South Carolinian by heritage born in New York in 1878 - his father's and grandfather's names were Charles Pinckney Bull - the third colonel in the story of The Tuleyries grew up in New Jersey and attended the U. S. Military Academy, receiving his appointment in 1897. After graduation in 1903, he served in the Philippines, returning in 1905. By 1907, he was again at West Point as a professor, and for the rest of his military career, rotated between infantry divisions and assignments at the Academy where he taught tactics and modern languages.

In 1917, Bull, by this time a captain, married Berenice Wyeth Furness, a young widow from St. Joseph, Missouri, who was described at the time as "St. Joe's wealthiest girl." They returned to West Point and in November of that year, he was promoted to major. By 1919, he had retired with the rank of Lieutenant Colonel. In 1921, the Bulls adopted a one-year-old girl whom they named Berenice and took home to Greenwich, Connecticut. Shortly thereafter, they agreed to disagree and in 1925, Berenice Bull married Col. Berkeley T. Merchant, another West Point graduate who had served as the chief veterinarian of the American Expeditionary Forces during World War I.

Georgette and Llewellyn were married at the home of her parents on May 18, 1930. They took up residence at Georgette's home nearby and spent their summers at The Tuleyries. Georgette continued her sculpture. Photographs of one of her classes survive as does a certificate dating from 1936 from The Grand Central School of Art which was located in the Grand Central Terminal. The school was founded in 1924 by painters Edmund Greacen, Walter Leighton Clark, and John Singer Sargent. During the twenty years of its operation, it

Lt. Col. Edmund Llewellyn Bull

had some 900 students running the gamut from Norman Rockwell to Willem de Kooning. A catalogue printed sometime after 1930 lists five separate schools: Painting & Drawing, Illustration, Design, Interior Design, and Sculpture.

The instructor in the School of Sculpture was Georg John Lober. He was born in Chicago in 1891 and spent most of his childhood in St. Louis. His father was a Danish immigrant who represented the Royal Copenhagen Porcelain Manufactory. The family moved to Keyport, New Jersey, while Lober was a teenager and it remained his home for the rest of his life. He trained as a sculptor at the National Academy of Design under Alexander Calder and was apprenticed to Gutzon Borglum, later sculptor of Mount Rushmore. A resolute practitioner of realism in his sculpture, Lober was honored by the Art Institute of Chicago, the Architectural League of New York, and the National Sculpture Society among others. He was appointed to the New York City Art Commission in 1942 and served as its Executive Secretary from 1943 until 1960. He is now best remembered for his bronzes of Hans Christian Andersen in Central Park and of George M. Cohan at the corner of West 47th Street and Seventh Avenue.

In the post-1930 catalogue, the entry describing the Sculpture School was in all likelihood written by Lober and noted that,

> *Classes in this department are held in our new Sculpture Studio in the Grand Central Terminal. This course has been arranged for students who wish to study sculpture seriously, and much stress is placed on the practical side of the profession, as well as the artistic side. We wish to discourage so-called "mantel-piece" sculpture and encourage a close relation between Architecture and Sculpture.*

Georgette was obviously a serious student of sculpture. By the time she received her "1st Honorable Mention for Portrait" certificate in 1936, she had been studying for at least ten years and had long since achieved sufficient skill to complete the bronze bust of Benito Quinquela Martin which she was so excited for her sister to see. She received another honorable that year, one in 1934, and a "special prize" for a Pan figure also in 1936. Years later, discarded plaster studies were still being discovered in outbuildings at The Tuleyries. Her interest in the art of others also continued. By 1929, she felt free to sell the Schreyer that Graham had bought when passing up the Titian and Rembrandt.

> *Did I write you that I have sold the Schreyer for $8,500 [Graham had paid $13,000] and had bought in its place a magnificent portrait of a lady (a Magdalene I think) 16th Century Flemish - a picture which I saw in Paris last autumn and fell in love with and had brought over on approval. I could not resist it though it cost more than the Schreyer sold for and I can't pay for it yet.*

Her interest was not limited to older periods. The 1929 will mentions a sculpture by Paul Manship, a protégé of her teacher, Georg Lober. The Bulls also maintained connections with others in the art world. Among the various entertaining and being entertained that went on

Above: The Sculpture Studio of The Grand Central School of Art. Georgette Bull is to the right of the model and instructor, Georg Lober, faces away from the model to the left

Below: Certificate awarded to Georgette in 1936

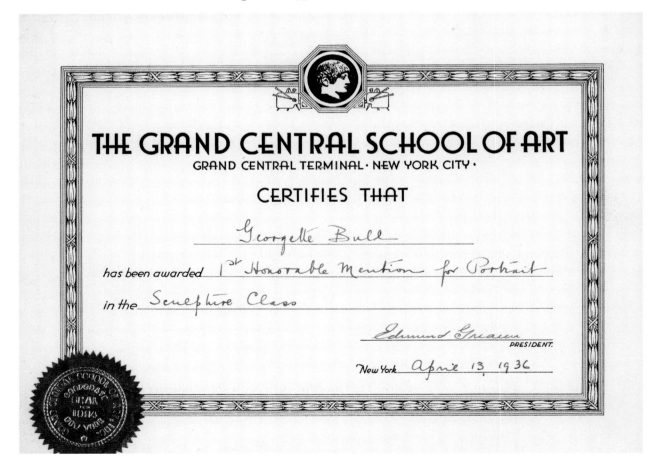

THE GRAND CENTRAL SCHOOL OF ART

GRAND CENTRAL TERMINAL · NEW YORK CITY ·

CERTIFIES THAT

Georgette Bull

has been awarded   1st Honorable Mention for Portrait

in the   Sculpture Class

Edmund Greacen
PRESIDENT.

New York   April 13, 1936

both in New York and Virginia, they hosted Baron Robert Doblhoff at The Tuleyries in 1931. The Baron was an Austrian who was well known for having painted portraits of notables up and down the East Coast, including Theodore Roosevelt's son-in-law, House Speaker Nicholas Longworth. Lober was also a frequent guest at The Tuleyries.

The Bulls regularly visited Hot Springs, Virginia, which seems to have been a spot favored by Orme and Elsie Wilson when they were in the United States. Llewellyn became a director of the Blue Ridge Country Club (which changed its name to the Millwood Country Club in the mid-1950s) and Georgette became a member of the Association for Preservation of Virginia Antiquities. In 1934, The Tuleyries began a long string of appearances on the annual Historic Garden Week tours sponsored by the Garden Club of Virginia.

The Tuleyries also became home to racehorses for the first time since *Blast* stood at stud for the Boyces. There is no prior hint that Georgette had any interest in the sport of kings but Llewellyn was a rider, probably from his days in the army. Regardless, Georgette was always listed as the owner of the horses. By the fall of 1931, a consignment was sent to the Timonium yearling sale. It appears that early in her marriage to Col. Bull, she purchased *Black Wand* and was delighted by the broodmare's record of 108 starts, placing in the money in 51 of them. The mare's sire was Col. E. R. Bradley's *Black Toney*, who sired 1924 Kentucky Derby winner *Black Gold,* and her dam was *Minawand*, later the dam of 1932 Kentucky Derby and Preakness winner *Burgoo King. Black Wand* became the foundation for the Bull's stable and produced a number of competent runners. In the spring of 1934, *Tuleyries Wand* campaigned at the nearby tracks at Bowie, Havre de Grace, and Cumberland and attending the races must have been a significant part of the Bulls' life. On June 30, 1939, her *Tuleyries Lin* ran in a claiming race at Delaware Park. This was clearly not a big-time operation but one which appears to have given both the Bulls pleasure and further connection to The Tuleyries.

From the evidence that survives, it appears that Georgette's prediction that her marriage to Llewellyn Bull "was no mistake" was accurate. Their lives together followed the seasonal migration between Manhattan and White Post. When at The Tuleyries, she continued to care for her garden, loved her dogs, and by all accounts led a more or less charmed life. Less than a month after *Tuleyries Lin* made his way around the track at Delaware Park, Georgette was dead at the young age of 53. The cause of her death on July 26, 1939, is remembered by the family as a ruptured esophagus while undergoing surgery in New York.

Four days after her marriage to Col. Bull, Georgette added a codicil to the 25-page will she had written a little over a year before. The first item of the document was a paragon of brevity, revoking the 1929 will and leaving everything she owned to her new husband. The second item was a bit longer.

> *In case my said husband shall not survive me or in case of our deaths simultaneously or if the order of our deaths cannot be determined or if my husband shall die in a common disaster with me or so nearly together with me that there shall not have been a reasonable time and opportunity to probate my said last Will and Testament and this Codicil thereto and thereby formally to establish rights thereunder, then and in either of those events I hereby give devise and bequeath all of my estate, whether real, personal or mixed and*

wherever situated, and all the rights and interests of every nature of or to which
I may die possessed or entitled, in accordance with the provisions of my said
Last Will and Testament, dated February 13, 1929.

This provision, clearly drafted by an attorney with a view of avoiding litigation down the road, failed in that purpose. On November 9, 1939, Llewellyn Bull died at The Tuleyries. Over the years of his marriage to Georgette and likely especially in the months following her death, he and Mrs. Borland had apparently become close and she traveled to Virginia to be with him during his final illness. His brother William wrote Elsie Wilson later that month that, "Mrs. Borland and I were with Llewellyn for the last few days before he died, and I shall never forget Mrs. Borland's kindness to him and her unfailing thoughtfulness and help. It was worth everything to my brother - and to me." Thus, within slightly more than three months of each other, he and Georgette joined the Tuleys and the Boyces at the Old Chapel Cemetery.

Col. Bull's will was executed on August 21, 1939. In it, he left everything he had inherited from Georgette to her sisters Elsie Wilson and Madeline Pell. There was also a bequest of $10,000 to his adopted daughter, Berenice Wyeth Bull. The remainder of his estate went to his brother William and his family. While all of this may seem simple enough, it provided gainful employment for a number of lawyers in Virginia and New York for some time thereafter.

Georgette Bull and one of her beloved Pekingeses with the mare, *Black Wand*

Orme Jr., Orme Sr., and Elsie Wilson with their cocker spaniel, Chief, at home on East 64th Street

THE WILSONS

Elsie Wilson ultimately became the sole owner and guardian of The Tuleyries through a deed in which she acquired the half interest of her sister, Madeline Pell. The deed was recorded on April 5, 1941. While it would seem obvious that a death in late July 1939 and a subsequent death in early November of the same year were hardly simultaneous, the validity of Georgette's 1930 codicil was litigated in her home state of New York where it was offered for probate. The matter was argued in the Surrogate's Court on June 28, 1940, and the judge rendered his decision on the matter two months later. As if to make sure there was no misunderstanding, the decision concludes:

> *FOUND, DETERMINED, ORDERED, ADJUDGED AND DECREED as follows:*
>
> *1. That the words in paragraph SECOND of the Codicil to decedent's will "Or if my husband shall die in a common disaster with me or so nearly together with me that there shall not have been a reasonable time and opportunity to probate my Last Will and Testament and this Codicil thereto and thereby formally to establish rights thereunder" define a single condition related only to the circumstances that would arise if fatal injuries had occurred both to the deceased and her husband in a common disaster and that said words have no relation to deaths occurring from so-called natural causes unrelated to violence or accidents affecting the testatrix or her husband; that in any event the interval between the date of death of deceased and the date of death of her husband constitute, as a matter of fact, a reasonable time and opportunity for the probate of deceased's testaments, and that therefore it was the intention of the testatrix, and the true construction and effect of her will and Codicil thereto is, that her surviving husband, E. Llewellyn Bull takes the entire estate of said decedent.*

As final as this order seems, some of the lawyers involved argued that the codicil should be construed in Virginia as well. Local counsel prevailed on this issue and as a result of this order, Col. Bull was determined to have owned The Tuleyries for three months in

1939, although by the time the decision was rendered he had been dead for nine months. As a result, the property passed under his will which prompted another round of litigation in Virginia and Maryland.

In 1921, Col. Bull and his first wife had adopted an infant girl and named her Berenice Wyeth Bull. Very soon thereafter the Bulls divorced and by 1927, the first Mrs. Bull had married Col. Berkeley Merchant. In his will, dated August 21, 1939, Bull left everything he received under Georgette's will to her sisters, Elsie and Madeline. He also left one-tenth, not to exceed $10,000.00, of the rest of his estate to his "adopted daughter, Berenice Wyeth Bull." The remaining nine-tenths went to his brother William who also served as an executor.

After Col. Merchant's retirement from the army, he and his family moved to Kensington, Maryland, and the younger Berenice assumed the name Merchant. Not satisfied with one-tenth up to $10,000.00 of Bull's estate, attorneys on her behalf challenged probate of his will on the grounds that he lacked mental capacity to make the will and that it was procured through undue influence.

On one level, it is easy to think of this action as grasping and demeaning to the memory of Col. Bull, especially given that the younger Berenice had recently made her debut at the Sulgrave Club in Washington as Berenice Merchant. On another, one feels considerable sympathy for her. Her father died in August 1939. She made her debut in December of that year. Litigation was ongoing about Bull's will in early 1940. Her mother died unexpectedly on April 13, 1940, nine days after eight witnesses had appeared in Clarke Circuit Court to attest to Bull's mental capacity and her attorney had been forced to withdraw his pleading.

Her mother's death prompted further litigation in St. Joseph, Missouri, in which her uncles and aunt sought a trust fund left by her grandfather Wyeth to her mother for life, remainder to her mother's "issue." The Wyeth siblings argued that the younger Berenice, who was adopted by the Bulls, was not the "issue" of her mother, Berenice Merchant, and that the trust should revert to them. The lower Federal court concluded that the term "issue" had the same meaning as "heirs of her body" and granted judgment to the Wyeths, leaving young Berenice nothing. The trial court's decision was affirmed by the U. S. Court of Appeals in June, 1941. Along the way, the *Billings Gazette* reported on November 9, 1940, that a marriage license had been issued for Clifford Longacre of Hardin, Montana, a small town near Billings, and Berenice Wyeth Bull of Kensington, Maryland. When all was said and done, the heirs of Col. Bull offered and obtained a release from Ms. Merchant and she ended up with $15,000.00 and a new husband. Sadly, she did not have the new husband for long as he was killed in fighting on the island of Peleliu in the Pacific in October, 1944, and was posthumously awarded the Silver Star for bravery.

Georgette Bull's death had also brought other provisions of Graham Blandy's will into effect. The remainder of his estate had been left in trust with the income to Georgette for life. At her death, the funds in trust were, after further legacies to his nephews, left to the University of Virginia. This and the initial success of the Blandy program helped Professor White undertake an expansion of the old Tuley slave quarters which tripled the size of the building and gave it a distinguished, campus-like appearance which it maintains today. A wing of roughly the dimensions of the quarters was built parallel to it and the two were joined by a third structure which featured an arcade facing the new court and a cupola above the central door. The stepped gables and porch of the original building were incorporated in the design and the whole was painted white like the buildings on the estate up the hill. In the process,

Arcade and porch of the main building at the Blandy Experimental Farm

White achieved his goal of making Blandy not only useful but beautiful. However, the coming of World War II soon put considerable strain on the program.

Orme and Elsie Wilson had been deeply involved in the developments leading up to World War II. They and their newborn son, Orme Jr., had set off for Europe in 1920. The birth of their only child on July 3, 1920, ten years after their marriage, had been a cause for rejoicing for the couple and the family. Young Orme was apparently a charmer from the beginning and photogenic besides and was soon given the nickname Bunny. An early story from their time in Bern tells that Bunny was accidentally locked in a hotel bathroom and had to be rescued by the members of the local fire department who were wielding axes. For some time thereafter, he refused to go anywhere without his hammer, the closest thing he could get to an ax. The experience made such an impression on everyone that a life-sized pastel portrait drawn at the time of the child holding his hammer hangs today at The Tuleyries.

Initial assignments for Orme Sr. included Bern and Brussels. When the Rogers Act created the career Foreign Service in 1924, he became one of its first officers. In 1927, Orme Sr. was assigned to Argentina and the family traveled to Buenos Aires. This was a very troubled time in that city, as in many others, due to the uproar relating to the conviction and planned execution of Italian anarchists Sacco and Vanzetti. An Italian immigrant to Argentina, Severino Di Giovanni, led a campaign of bombings in Buenos Aires, targeting first the American Embassy on May 16, 1926, following the refusal of the Supreme Court of Massachusetts to grant the pair a new trial. Other attacks focused on American banks in the city and an attempt to bomb the train in which President Herbert Hoover was riding on a visit to the country in 1928.

Elsie and Orme Jr. happened to be in the lobby of one of the targeted banks when a bomb was tossed through the doors. Elsie pushed her son and a nearby child under a table and fell on top of them. The bomb failed to explode but the story caused great concern when it reached the family back home. Madeline Pell wrote to Elsie in an undated letter from Biarritz about this time that, "Ma very worried all the time about you and B. A. with the Sacco-V. bombs Little Nels said how could you stop them winging bombs at Aunt Elsie from here?" A chilling photograph of Orme Jr. aboard his bicycle with guards standing nearby tells part of the story.

Orme Sr. holds Bunny who holds his hammer

Following his time in Buenos Aires, Orme Sr. returned to Washington and rose through the ranks to become Assistant Chief of the Latin American Division. In 1933, he was sent to Berlin as First Secretary of the American Embassy and in late 1934 was posted to Prague as Consul General. After again serving in Buenos Aires in 1937 and 1938, he returned to Brussels where the ambassador was Joseph E. Davies, former head of the Interstate

Commerce Commission and previously ambassador to the Soviet Union, who had the added advantage of being married to Marjorie Merriweather Post. Davies' mission to Brussels ended in November, 1939, and he was succeeded by Joseph C. Cudahy who had previously served as ambassador to Poland and Ireland. Following the German invasion of Belgium beginning on May 28, 1940, Cudahy left Brussels in July. Orme Sr., as Chargé d'Affaires, oversaw the evacuation of the embassy when instructed by the Germans to leave and returned to Washington.

Elsie accompanied Mr. Wilson at all these posts as did Orme Jr. until he entered St. Mark's School in Southborough, Massachusetts, in 1933. Thereafter, he spent summers with his parents. Elsie's primary activities were looking after Orme Jr. and supporting her husband's efforts in the diplomatic arena but all was not work. A photograph from a Berlin newspaper which ran in 1934 shows Elsie with other diplomatic wives as part of *Ein Hunde-Club der Berliner Diplomatenfrauen*, a group which seems to have regularly gathered for exercise and conversation in the Tiergarten.

By the time Orme Sr. evacuated Brussels, Elsie had already returned to America and Orme Jr. had graduated from St. Mark's and matriculated to Harvard, class of 1942. From an early age, he was both enamored with his highly athletic Pell cousins and somewhat skeptical of his parents' devotion to the arts. During his time at Harvard, he participated in the Navy ROTC program, played varsity squash, and was elected captain of the tennis team his senior year.

Orme Jr. in Buenos Aires, 1927 or 1928

Ein Hunde-Club der Berliner Diplomatenfrauen, 1934, with Elsie Wilson standing fourth from the left

As her husband was dealing with the outbreak of World War II and her son was off at college, Elsie was dealing with the aftermath of the Bulls' deaths and taking on the challenge of owning and managing The Tuleyries. Many years later, she recalled her first arrival in a brochure for one of the many garden tours which have visited the estate over the years.

> *In 1908 Mr. Blandy married my older sister, Georgette. Two months after the wedding I boarded a night train in New York, and was on my way to visit The Tuleyries. The following morning at Shenandoah Junction I changed to another train for Boyce, Va. The last three miles of the trip were made in a horse-drawn contraption of The Tuleyries, the place with which I immediately fell in love. I had never seen anything like it before! The house, the grounds, and all the buildings were enchanting. I loved the grass driveways, the orchards, and the open fields to run across. Going to the old icehouse to get ice from under the saw dust was an adventure, or seeing the incubated chickens burst out of their shells. I remember moonlight on the marble floored patico at night, the summerhouse in the garden covered with Hiawatha roses, and the masses of flowers. My sister divided a part of the garden into twelve flower beds, around which she planted boxwood clippings. This boxwood has now grown so large that it almost covers the paths separating the flower beds.*

Neither Elsie's love for The Tuleyries nor her devotion to Georgette's memory ever waned and she was vigilant in protecting and preserving the estate as she had received it. Her attachment was doubtless increased by the fact that there was a stability there which she did not find elsewhere in her life. Family lore repeats that she "set up housekeeping" 36 times during her life and even when in the U. S., she and Orme Sr. traveled between their

Orme Jr. and Elsie

home in New York and one at 2406 Massachusetts Avenue in Washington. From the time she became owner of The Tuleyries, she spent the summers at White Post until she turned 98, unless she was out of the country. While her husband was stationed in Washington focusing on Latin American affairs during most of World War II, she was battling the Virginia highway department over the reconstruction of U. S. 50 through a portion of the farm and the resulting condemnation action.

On March 21, 1944, the aspiration of every Foreign Service officer was fulfilled for Orme Sr. when he was appointed by President Roosevelt as Ambassador Extraordinary and Plenipotentiary to Haiti. He and Elsie took up residence in Port-au-Prince and he presented his credentials to the Haitian government on June 2. With two decades of diplomatic service under her own belt, Elsie threw herself into various charitable endeavors on the island including work at clinics established to treat yaws, a highly contagious bacterial skin disease which thrived in the tropics in general and Haiti in particular at the time. Her work was recognized by the nation when she was awarded the *Ordre National de l'Honneur et du Mérite*. One of her friends wrote of her that, "I know no one except Eleanor Roosevelt who can crowd into one day all you can. She at least usually goes early to bed which you apparently do not."

Upon graduation from Harvard, Orme Jr. enlisted in the U. S. Navy and began training as an aviator. Upon completion of his training he was sent to Iowa and later to Texas and Florida as a flight instructor for much of the war. Somewhere along the way, he crossed paths with Julie Brown Colt, a divorced actress several years his senior. She was the adopted daughter of Mr. and Mrs. Philip Marshall Brown. He was a distinguished diplomat and later professor at Princeton. On February 15, 1945, they were married at the Naval Air Station in Daytona Beach, her mother and his parents being the only guests.

Referring to Orme Jr. as "the lieutenant," Gwynne Jones wrote to Elsie two weeks following the wedding, "They certainly have my best wishes for a congenial + happy voyage through this vail of eternal problems." It was not to be and, although she gave birth in 1946 to a son, Marshall, the marriage soon ended.

Gwynne Harrison Page Jones was the long-time farm manager of The Tuleyries during most of Elsie's reign. He is remembered as taking the job in 1942, having previously been employed at nearby Pagebrook Stud. He and his family, which included two sons and two daughters, moved onto the property in 1944. He had a long-standing interest in thoroughbreds, their bloodlines, breeding, and conformation, and competed as an amateur steeplechase rider in his youth. His family had deep roots in Clarke County and maintained its own farm until the 1960s. He was a fixture in the local community, serving as an officer of the Farm Bureau, on the Clarke County planning commission from 1956 to 1979 (its chairman for many of those years), and actively participating in local theatrical productions.

Like the Blandys and H. L. Martin, Elsie relied on Jones to keep the place operating and in order while she was either out of the country or away for the winter months. In addition to looking after the horses on the property, Jones oversaw a general farming operation that included Angus cattle, Galloway belted and Poland pigs, sheep, chickens, and a few dairy cows, as well as raising the corn and hay necessary to feed all those animals. There was also an extensive vegetable garden and the remnants of Graham Blandy's orchards. Members of the local Brisco, Dabney, and Washington families worked on the farm and Bertha Brisco and Julia Washington helped Elsie in the main house during the summers.

Elsie and Gwynne both seem to have taken a rather fatalistic view of life but Jones clearly had his sentimental side as well. In another letter penned in 1945, he wrote that, "This morning Gwynne Jr. and I took a lovely lot of flowers down to the 'Old Chapel' and put them on Colonel + Mrs. Bull's graves as we felt sure you and Mrs. Borland would like it done - they were the only Spring flowers in the Cemetery."

Years later, in 1976, Elsie deeded to Jones and his wife, Susan Randolph Jones, the home they had occupied at The Tuleyries and the 22.64 acres upon which it sat.

Even though written with legal formality, the deed expressed what it may not have been possible to say in person between these two. Further consideration was described as Elsie's "respect for Gwynne H. Jones and in appreciation of the loyalty and services of said Gwynne H. Jones." The Joneses had four children, including among them a lieutenant colonel in the Air Force, an electrical engineer, and a college professor. Their grandson, Dr. Page Jones, and his family continue to live in the home next to The Tuleyries today.

After President Roosevelt's death in 1945, he was succeeded by his Vice President, Harry S. Truman. He had his own man for Port-au-Prince and Ambassador Wilson's assignment ended on August 22, 1946. Having reached the mandatory retirement age of 60 by that time, he left the Foreign Service and settled into life in New York, Washington, and White Post, pursuing his goal "to expand the mind and refine the sensibilities." It is said that he was deathly bored at The Tuleyries and spent his afternoons there clipping Georgette's boxwood. Service on the boards of the National Cathedral, Washington's Children's Hospital, and the Seaman's Church Institute in New York was much more to his taste than rural Virginia. His love of music manifested itself in contributions to the development of the Kennedy Center in Washington and the construction of the Metropolitan Opera House at Lincoln Center. The Corcoran Gallery of Art was also the object of his generosity. He maintained his connections to the Foreign Service, acting as one of the seven incorporators of the Diplomatic and Consular Officers, Retired or DACOR in 1952, an organization which continues to promote the interests of former members of the diplomatic corps.

Elsie, who religiously attended the opera every week when in New York, loved The Tuleyries and was equally at home there. She was as adept at canning peaches, making wine in the basement, and picnicking in the garden as she had been in managing the six gardeners, two chauffeurs, three housemen, two housemaids, cook, kitchen maid, and two laundresses who were attached to the ambassadorial residence in Haiti. Hogs were raised on the farm so that Mr. Jones could smoke hams. Incubating chicks continued to break through their shells. There were cows for milking and sheep roamed the fields.

After the conclusion of the war, Orme Jr. continued to fly, both in the Naval Reserve and as a commercial pilot for Pan American Airways. He also pursued his interest in geography which had been his concentration at Harvard. He was employed at the U. S. Army Map Service and began work on a master's in the subject at George Washington University, focusing on Clarke County. While he was finishing the master's thesis and degree, he married Mildred Eddy Dunn on February 16, 1950, at St. John's Church on Lafayette Square in Washington. She was the daughter of Mildred Eddy and William McKee Dunn.

Mildred, or Midge as she was universally known, was born in Paris on July 17, 1922, while her parents were visiting the city on leave from her father's duties in Germany. Ultimately a brigadier general and grandson of another brigadier general and congressman of the same name, Dunn was serving as an aide-de-camp to the general in charge of American occupying forces in the Rhineland. Midge grew up in Washington and at her family's idyllic country house, Gramercy, outside Hot Springs, Virginia. In 1940, she graduated from the Foxcroft School in Middleburg and after the United States entered World War II she joined the American Red Cross and served at an airbase in Tampa, Florida. In 1945, she boarded the RMS *Queen Elizabeth* along with some 10,000 soldiers heading to Europe. Although attacked by German submarines en route, she and they arrived safely and she began service with the Red Cross in England, Belgium, and France. While in Europe, she crossed paths

Orme Wilson Jr.

Mildred Eddy Dunn Wilson

with her father who served as military attaché to the Allied Governments in Exile in London and later as military attaché in Brussels.

The Dunn and Wilson families were friends, noted several times as dining together at the Homestead in the social pages of the inter-war years. Orme Jr. and Midge apparently became an item after Midge suffered a badly broken leg while skiing at Stowe, Vermont, in 1948. She was transferred to a Washington hospital for recovery and as the story goes, Elsie "strongly encouraged" her son to pay Midge a visit while she was recuperating. The visit turned into bridge games at the hospital and, after her release, outings to the races and ballgames followed. On an outing along the scenic Skyline Drive atop the Blue Ridge, Orme Jr. asked Midge to marry him.

They made a dashing couple. Marriage to Midge was not the only decision Orme Jr. made in 1950. He passed the Foreign Service examination and followed his father's footsteps into the diplomatic corps. By that time, he had also begun another lifelong passion, horse racing. His first posting with the State Department was as a consular officer in Frankfurt, Germany. From there in May 1951 he sought permission to race *Astrodome* and *Fair Beacon* at Delaware Park. The report ran in the Wilmington, Delaware, and Lancaster, Pennsylvania, papers, the former calling his proposed entries "a pair of useful, if not eminent, horses." Even more exciting in what must have seemed an *annus mirabilis*, their first child, Elsie Dunn Wilson, was born in Washington on December 8, 1950.

Orme Jr. shared his father's deep commitment to public service and the desire to travel the world and learn ever more about it. Although he was never appointed as an ambassador, he had that latter desire fulfilled several times over. After Frankfurt, he and Mildred, Marshall (nicknamed Ricky), Elsie, and Orme III, born on October 28, 1952, moved to Southampton, England, where he was again posted to the consulate. They returned to Washington in 1955 and in 1957 he was sent to Columbia University to learn to speak the Serbo-Croatian language in preparation for his posting in the political section of the U. S. Embassy in Belgrade, Yugoslavia. The years 1961 to 1964 found them in Athens, Greece.

For something completely different, Orme Jr. was then sent to the Air War College in Montgomery, Alabama, after which he served in various assignments in Washington. In 1970, the family returned to Yugoslavia, this time to Zagreb where he served as Consul General. Home again from 1974 to 1977, he was posted to the U. S. Mission to the United Nations, serving with Ambassadors John A. Scali, Daniel Patrick Moynihan, William Scranton, and Andrew Young. His final assignment with the Foreign Service - which then required retirement at age 60 - was back to Europe where he was Political Counselor at the U. S. Mission to NATO from 1977 to 1980, thus completing a career in which he served with distinction at senior levels of the Foreign Service in some of the world's most sensitive locations.

While the younger Wilsons were moving hither and yon, Elsie and Orme Sr. enjoyed their retirement. The first major change in their life was the decision in the mid-1950s to part with the home they had built on East 64th and take an apartment on Park Avenue. Soon thereafter, Elsie's mother, Alice Borland, died at age 96 on July 19, 1959. With the closing of the Borland home in Manhattan, a fascinating collection of portraits made their way to The Tuleyries. The most prominent is a three-quarter length portrait of King George II. Tradition holds that it was presented to Dr. James Lloyd, an ancestor of Elsie's, by British officers evacuating Boston in 1776 in recognition for his services in treating British soldiers during the smallpox

Marshal Tito, Madame Broz, Midge Wilson, and Consul General Wilson in Zagreb, Yugoslavia

King George II, attributed to John Shackleton

epidemics which had raged in the city. Long thought to be the work of Sir Godfrey Kneller, the Frick Digital Collection now describes it as a copy of a Kneller by John Shackleton who was Painter in Ordinary or court painter to George II from 1749 until his death in 1767. As Kneller died in 1723 and George did not ascend to the throne until 1727, it is now accepted that the King posed for Shackleton sometime in the 1740s and that the painter produced a number of similar portraits of the King in the years that followed.

A very similar image of the King, part of the British Royal Collection, hangs in the Ambassador's Entrance at Buckingham Palace and was purchased by William IV from the Pownall Estate in 1835. Thomas Pownall, governor of the Massachusetts Bay Colony from 1757 to 1760, purchased a version of the painting from Shackleton in July 1757 for 55 pounds. Thomas having died childless in 1805, his estate passed to his nephew, George, who died in 1834, also without issue. It was from his estate that that portrait made its way, first to Windsor and later to Buckingham Palace. One wonders if Thomas Pownall actually purchased two copies and had one shipped to Massachusetts. Regardless of its actual origin, Dr. Lloyd's portrait of the King has hung in the entry hall of The Tuleyries for sixty years.

One can have dinner by oneself and never be alone in the dining room at The Tuleyries. Dr. Lloyd's son, Massachusetts Senator James Lloyd, hangs above one of the fireplaces. On the opposite wall his grandfather, Henry, and Henry's mother and father-in-law, John and Elizabeth Tailer Nelson, stare sternly assuring any doubters that the Borlands had very

The dining room with three of the Nelson-Lloyd family portraits

deep New England roots. A portrait attributed to John Wesley Jarvis of General John Armstrong Jr., Secretary of War under Madison, ambassador to France, and kin from the other side of the family, hangs over the other mantel.

It is fascinating to think what the Lloyds and Nelsons, let alone what Blandy, would have thought about the goings on at the Blandy Experimental Farm around this time. During the tenure of W. Ralph Singleton as Director of the farm from 1955 to 1965, various experiments were carried out in conjunction with the Atomic Energy Commission. In 1957, he and an assistant designed and installed a radiation pit lined with concrete into which cobalt could be raised from its housing. The effects of radiation at different distances and for different lengths of time were observed on various plants, primarily corn. Elsie was not initially pleased with this development but was sufficiently reassured by Dr. Singleton that she raised no objections. The same could not be said when, after Dr. Singleton's retirement in 1965, the university considered closing the program and possibly selling the property. Corresponding with everyone from her neighbor, Virginia Senator Harry F. Byrd, to the university's president, she became a formidable advocate for her late brother-in-law's legacy. Whether her efforts had any effect on the situation will never really be known but the Blandy Experimental Farm and Virginia State Arboretum continue to thrive today.

Although less exciting, another development at Blandy had as much impact on its long-term survival. In 1961, The American Boxwood Society was formed and made its headquarters at the farm, bringing it to the attention and affections of its members. Elsie served on its first board of directors. The ubiquitous shrub itself added to the luster of Blandy's name in the horticultural world. A fastigiate cultivar identified at the farm in 1949 was named *Buxus sempervirens* 'Graham Blandy.' Reaching a height of nine feet and recipient of a Royal Horticultural Society Award of Merit, the cultivar is often used in American gardens to provide the vertical emphasis provided by the Italian cypress in warmer climes.

Despite the various happenings at Blandy, little changed at The Tuleyries and this became a bone of contention between Elsie and Orme Jr. His interest in racehorses that had continued to grow over the years was in the blood. His great-uncle, Richard Thornton Wilson Jr., had been part of the group which revived the Saratoga racetrack in the 1890s and he later raced 1901 Preakness winner *The Parader* and 1922 Preakness and Belmont winner *Pillory*. Georgette had taken up racing after Blandy's death and, as a teenager visiting the farm, Orme Jr. would have been familiar with her horses and their training.

Robert Frost famously said that good fences make good neighbors and good fences are even more important for thoroughbreds. As she grew older, Elsie Wilson is said to have become more and more like her New England ancestors and less likely to change anything at The Tuleyries, including the fences. This led Orme Jr., despite her disapproval, to purchase the adjacent 220 acres northwest of The Tuleyries and name it Westfield Farm in 1966, the year of Ambassador Wilson's death. He proceeded to have a modern twelve-stall barn and various run-in sheds constructed on the property, aiming to make it a professional breeding and racing operation. Soon thereafter, his home-bred colt *Tatoi* proved a *very* useful, if not eminent member of the stable, placing in the money in twenty-three of his thirty-six starts between 1969 and 1972 and making it to the winner's circle ten times. He was then retired to stud at nearby Newstead Farm. From 1980 to 1982, *Gilded Age* placed in the money eighteen of his thirty-one races, winning eight, including the Grade III Longfellow Handicap at Monmouth Park in New Jersey. This colt, one of the few horses in Orme Jr.'s

"Tatoi"
at Newstead Farm
by Wallace W. Nall, III,
1923-2003

"Gilded Age"
by Wallace W. Nall, III,
1923-2003

Orme III, Orme Jr., Frank Y. Whiteley Jr., and Gwynne Jones at the trophy presentation after *Tatoi* won The Dover Stakes at Delaware Park on July 4, 1969

stable which was not home grown, had been purchased late in his racing career with the goal of strengthening the breeding stock in Virginia.

Orme Jr.'s success with his horses was not a one-man show. In the late 1960s, he hired a full-time farm manager for Westfield, Fred Myer, who lived on the farm with his family for over two decades. Gwynne Jones, remembered as "knowing everything about horses", continued to provide expert advice over the years, especially when the Wilsons were overseas or posted elsewhere in the United States. Orme Jr. was also assisted by the accomplished team of trainer Frank Y. Whiteley Jr., a Maryland native who during his career trained 1965 Preakness winner *Tom Rolfe* and 1967 Preakness and Belmont winner *Damascus*, as well as the famous filly *Ruffian* and many more. In 1978, Whiteley was inducted into the National Museum of Racing Hall of Fame.

While Orme Jr. pursued his career and racing interests, his mother continued to spend every summer at The Tuleyries until she turned 98. Up until that time, she had remained incredibly active and in charge of the Virginia estate. At 90, she and a friend went on safari to Tanzania and at 94, shortly after suffering a broken hip, she traveled to China. Nearing her one-hundredth birthday and living in New York full time, her health began to weaken but she rallied for a grand family celebration of the centenary of her birth in New York on April 7, 1987. After reaching that remarkable milestone, she continued to decline and died on December 2, 1987. She was laid to rest with Ambassador Wilson in his family's mausoleum in the Woodlawn Cemetery in the Bronx.

For the first time in its history, The Tuleyries passed without further complication to its next owner, Georgette's nephew and Elsie's only child, Orme Jr., who spent the next year figuring out exactly what to do with it. The answer he and Midge settled on was to part with Elsie's New York apartment and focus on The Tuleyries. That required a major restoration upon which they soon embarked. It is suggested by some that Orme Jr. undertook the project, less for love of the house than from a sense of duty and family obligation. Given the care he lavished upon the project, to say nothing of the financial resources, it is difficult for an outsider to see anything but a deep and abiding appreciation and affection for the old house and farm. Over the years it may have become dark and dusty, cluttered with hunting trophies and other accretions, and have always been hot when the family visited in the summer, but this clearly did not stop him from seeing what it had been and could again become or having the commitment to see the project through. At the deepest level, it may have been an innate feeling that anything which had survived 150 years should have the chance to survive for another 150.

One of the younger Wilson's first projects had actually begun shortly before his mother's death. In a letter dated May 10, 1990, headed "To Whom It May Concern", and signed by him as Executor, he described how the designation of the Blandy Experimental Farm as The State Arboretum of Virginia in 1986 had prompted his mother to be concerned about both the appearance of and lack of security provided by the dry-laid stone walls on The Tuleyries property. At Elsie's request, Orme Jr. contacted George White Fencing, Inc., of Middleburg which provided an estimate of $20 per foot to repair the walls. Elsie agreed and White began work on November 13, 1987. The first portions of the walls to be addressed were those between the house and Blandy and some 3,250 feet of wall were repaired by spring of 1988. For this work, White came in within 50 cents per foot of his estimate.

There was that much more work to be done and some of the walls to the north and west of the house were as much as eight feet tall. By the time Orme Jr. wrote his letter in the spring of 1990, presumably as part of settling his mother's estate, White had repaired an additional 6,973 feet of wall and the higher walls meant higher prices. This work averaged $29.78 per foot. All in all, almost two miles of walls were restored at a cost of over $250,000.

To defray some of this expense, deal with trees which had grown into the fences, and complete some general upkeep on the grounds, Orme Jr. sold timber in 1988. Things needed doing at the house as well. The passage of 150 years since its construction and the weight of the concrete poured on the second-story floors during Blandy's initial modernization had caused cracks and bulges in the masonry structure which, if left unaddressed, threatened the integrity of the walls. When the house was built, the joists for the second floor were run parallel to the hall walls, presumably to avoid the chimneys in those walls. This meant that

Repairing the dry-laid stone walls in 1988

The Tuleyries in scaffolding in the spring of 1990

the joists from the front and rear rooms met above the arch for the great doors separating those rooms. Later, when the Boyces removed the wall between the two first-floor rooms to the right of the hall and Blandy constructed a bath above the new arch and inserted a new window for that bath, the situation on that side of the house became particularly troubling. There had also been miscellaneous instances of water damage which needed to be repaired.

To oversee the needed work, the Wilsons retained John Milner, an internationally known architect specializing in historic preservation who was working at nearby Audley Farm at the time. During 1988, his firm prepared an extensive condition report on the house which became the basis for the proposed work which was sent on December 5, 1988. The Wilsons and Milner, assisted by Christina Henry (now Carter), worked through the year 1989 completing the details for the restoration, and floor plans were delivered in December. On February 12, 1990, the Wilsons entered a contract with Wood-Tech Construction Co., Inc., of Berryville which called for substantial completion of the project by October 31, 1990. By March, the house was surrounded by scaffolding as work progressed. The project was a matter of great local interest, *The Winchester Star* reporting on March 30, 1990, under the headline "Save a Mansion - It's a Clarke Mission", that the project was expected to cost $485,000. As it turned out, that figure was some $100,000 short and the project took longer than anticipated because of the financial difficulties of the contractor. By late 1990, Wood-Tech was insolvent and Orme Jr. in effect became the general contractor on the job.

A constant presence in the restoration and ever since has been the foreman, Marcel Bousquet. A master craftsman and construction manager, he had built and restored various buildings across the country from California to Virginia. His care and attention to The Tuleyries has ensured that all the work done during the restoration has continued to be maintained to the highest standards. From his workshop behind the main house, he continued until 2020 to keep an eagle eye on the place which he and his wife, Ruth, treated almost as another child.

It was decided early on that the restoration would not attempt to undo the changes made to the house over the years but would be focused on correcting structural problems that had been caused by those changes. As a result, one of the top priorities was installing steel beams over the doors separating the parlors and above the arch which the Boyces had inserted between the two rooms to the right of the hall when they converted them into their dining room and ballroom. This provided much-needed support for the baths on the second floor but required removal of all the woodwork on these walls and its eventual reinstallation. To accomplish this without anyone being able to tell it had been done, Milner and his team were assisted by Gary Gredell of Wilmington, Delaware, a structural engineer known for his discreet interventions in historic buildings.

The other priority was removal of the concrete which had been poured over the original flooring on the second floor to encase plumbing pipes for the added baths. This had then been covered with new flooring. Once both the new but 80-year-old flooring and the concrete had been removed, the original floor was removed and the joists, which had sagged under the weight, were sistered and the original floors reinstalled. All of this had to be done, as the saying goes, *very* carefully to avoid damage to the ceilings of the double parlors and their elaborate plaster cornices and medallions which were in precarious condition. Grid hangers and epoxy were used to stabilize them after the floor work above was completed. In the original bathrooms themselves, the existing fixtures were replumbed and reused as

Opposite:
Above left: one of several cracks in the exterior masonry caused by excess weight on the second floor

Below left: completing installation of the steel beam between the parlors

Above right: leaded sidelight before restoration

Below right: sistered floor joists in the southeast bedroom on the second floor

This page:
Above: arch below new steel beam in the center of the dining room

Below: Marcel Bousquet, foreman for the original restoration who continued to look after The Tuleyries until 2020

designed by Mantle Fielding, consistent with the approach of maintaining the house as it had evolved over time.

Outside, wind, water, sun, and woodpeckers had taken a toll on the woodwork over the years. It was found that the columns on the south portico were actually oak tree trunks onto which the fluting was veneered. As needed, the fluted veneer was removed, repaired or copied, and replaced. Similar work occurred on the cornices and where water had damaged the rafter tails and they were sistered as well. The leaded fan and sidelights around the entry doors were removed and completely restored. Deteriorating woodwork was repaired on the cupola and dampers were installed in the four great chimneys with their dozen flues. In a move that was doubtless considered heretical to some at the time, Milner insisted on removing all the boxwood from around the foundation of the house to improve drainage.

While most of the work done by Milner and the contractors was meant not to be seen, much effort and consideration went into planning the kitchen in the pantry behind the dining room and the addition of baths on both floors of the conservatory wing. Along with retaining John Milner, the Wilsons hired Sally Worthington Interior Design, Inc., of Charlottesville to assist with refurnishing the home once construction was completed. Ms. Worthington, who specialized in renovation of old houses, assisted in culling the contents of the old house which did not appear to have been emptied since the time of the Tuleys.

Many items of antique kitchen and laundry equipment were donated to Maymont in Richmond. Much of the existing furniture was recovered but several pieces, including the Victorian etageres, were donated to the White House of the Confederacy. All of the original woodwork in the house was painted cream as were the Boyces' ceiling beams in the dining room. After much consideration, the height of the paneling in the dining room was lowered more than a foot but it was left unpainted. The Boyces' ornate overmantels were removed and relegated to the Porter Lodge, making way for the portraits of Senator Lloyd and General Armstrong.

While the parlor walls received a coat of soft yellow paint to make the doors and woodwork stand out, the rest of the rooms were painted in the same cream. Pattern was added by an antique Aubusson in the front parlor and a Tabriz in the rear parlor where modern upholstery picked up the dark blues and burnt oranges of the rug. A massive dark red Afghan Ersari rug anchors the dining room which is warmed by the Boyces' paneling and the beautiful mahogany doors. In the bedrooms, muted florals in scale with the size and height of the rooms were used for curtains from the workroom of Nelson Beck in Washington, dust ruffles, and upholstery.

All of this was in keeping with what Ms. Worthington described as the conservative taste of the Virginians with whom she worked and reflected the continuing influence of the Colonial Revival and International Movement on restoration of historic properties throughout much of the 20th century. With the intention to maintain the house much as it had been for the past eighty years, no effort was made to determine if there were historic paints or remnants of the flamboyant papers which no doubt decorated the walls during the 19th century.

Other family treasures made their way to The Tuleyries and added to the mix. A lovely oil of the salon at Elsie's mother-in-law's home in Manhattan by American artist Walter Gay (1856-1937) made its way to an honored place in the front parlor at The Tuleyries. The *secrétaire à abbatant* seen in the painting, with its exquisite marquetry, and the pair

Walter Gay painting of the salon at 3 East 64th Street, Manhattan

of Chinese figurines seen gracing the chest in the painting found a new home in one of the upstairs bedrooms. Other fine French furniture found a home in the entry hall while the Boyces' pier mirror still hung between the front windows in the front parlor. The result was something of an oxymoron, grandly comfortable and above all, beautiful and fascinating.

As work progressed on the house, plans were also afoot to begin restoration of the farm buildings, particularly those in the quadrangle. On March 13, 1991, Orme Jr. signed an agreement with Milner for an assessment of the work that would be needed on these buildings but it was not to be. His work on the mansion virtually complete, Orme Jr. died suddenly in the early hours of March 30, 1991, of a heart attack. The upholsterers were called to bring the furniture which had been waiting for placement at the house and, instead of celebrating a remarkable accomplishment, Midge and the children instead received friends at The Tuleyries to mourn his passing. It was clearly not the gathering anyone anticipated inaugurating a new era at The Tuleyries. Orme Jr. was buried at the Gramercy Farm Cemetery on the Dunn family property outside Hot Springs, Virginia.

Orme Jr. and Midge Wilson with Annie during the 1989-1991 restoration of The Tuleyries

Throughout his retirement, Orme Jr. had pursued his racing interests. In 1990, two of his horses were beginning successful careers on the track. *Ritchie Trail* campaigned from 1990 to 1994 and won seven of her forty-five starts, placing in the money a total of twenty-seven times. *Gilded Youth*, the son of Wilson's *Gilded Age*, had a longer career, racing from 1990 to 1998 and winning ten of his forty-five races while finishing in the money in a total of twenty-four.

In 1989, Orme Jr. received the Virginia Breeder of the Year award from the Thoroughbred Owners and Breeders Association. As a member of the Virginia Racing Commission's Advisory Task Force, he was instrumental in bringing pari-mutuel betting to Virginia tracks. In 1991, he was president of the Virginia Thoroughbred Association (VTA) and earlier had served on the board of Maryland's Laurel Race Course. Sadly, he did not live to receive the Award of Distinction presented by *SPUR* magazine or to enjoy his induction into VTA's Virginia Equine Hall of Fame in 2001.

Wilson had also been instrumental in 1984 in organizing the Friends of Blandy to support the ongoing programs at the neighboring property. After serving as its first president, he later was on its board of directors for a number of years. The group became the Foundation of the State Arboretum or FOSA in 1989. After his death, a new flagpole at the entrance to the main building was erected in his honor near the gazebo that had been named for his mother.

At the time of his death, Orme Jr. and Midge were living in the apartment originally intended for a trainer in the stable at Westfield. Midge never left it. She continued the farm's breeding business, raced its horses into the early 2000s, and continued to look after them until her death in 2017. She never moved into The Tuleyries. Various explanations have been given: it was too large for one person; it was too expensive to heat in the winter; it was too hot in the summer (Milner had advised against installing air conditioning, saying that the huge windows and cupola would keep it cool in the summer); etc. One suspects it was simply too sad to leave the spot where she and her husband had enjoyed the height of their racing activity and overseen the restoration of the main house, and even sadder to be in the house where the most immediate memory would have been receiving friends to mourn his passing.

Whatever the reason, The Tuleyries slipped back into another quarter-century when little changed. It was carefully maintained with the help of the restoration foreman, Marcel Bousquet, who worked from the large basement kitchen and well-equipped workshop in the garage until 2020. The grand house was used for family gatherings and the Garden Club came to visit but it was otherwise allowed another long slumber. Like her mother-in-law before her, Midge remained in complete control of the farm until her death on November 30, 2017, at the age of 95. She was buried next to Orme Jr. at the Gramercy Farm Cemetery on a cold, gray morning with the wind racing around the mountains of her beloved Gramercy. Friends and family gathered the next day to remember her at Christ Church in Millwood, the town where the first Joseph Tuley began his successful career so many years before.

Elsie, Orme Jr., Orme III, and Midge Wilson aboard the S. S. *Atlantic* on their way to Athens in 1961

E PILOGUE

Elsie Thompson and Orme Wilson III inherited The Tuleyries upon their mother's death in 2017. Both Harvard educated like their father and grandfather Wilson before them, they have established lives away from Clarke County. Orme III, known as Sandy to family and friends, and his wife, Mary Hilliard, live in Mary's hometown, Louisville, Kentucky, where his career included stints in banking and owning printing companies. Their only child, a daughter, and her husband live on the West Coast.

Elsie, like her mother, attended Foxcroft, then Radcliffe College and the University of Virginia School of Law. She met her husband, William McIlwaine Thompson Jr. of Richmond, Virginia, another Virginia law school graduate, when both were working in Houston, Texas. They have made their home in Charlottesville and their two sons and two daughters all live in the Northeast.

Rather than have The Tuleyries again return to amber for an indeterminate period of time, Elsie and Sandy embarked on a substantial campaign of maintenance and updating and, having the place in pristine condition, decided that it was time for the long family ownership begun by Graham Blandy to come to an end. On August 10, 2020, Robert Maxwell Emma and his wife, Ruth Rhodes Emma, became the latest owners of The Tuleyries. This book tells the story of the grand house and farm up to that date. All who are familiar with this landmark of the Old Dominion devoutly hope that it will have a happy and prosperous future as new chapters in its history are written.

Orme Jr. with Annie

AUTHOR'S NOTE

The Tuleyries marks the second time I have been asked by its owners to write the story of a historic property. The first was the Beaumont Inn in Harrodsburg, Kentucky, and I was commissioned by Centre classmates to celebrate the centennial of their family's ownership of the Inn which had previously been a girl's college and a frontier spa. In that book, I noted that the process was an unalloyed pleasure and the same has been true at The Tuleyries.

One of the great pleasures of such a project is delving deeply into the history of the place and the various people who have made it their business or home. There is also the opportunity to spend more time in a building than one can when it is not one's own. No brief visit can give the feel that spending extended periods of time in it can. However, the best part is spending time with friends and in the process, not only getting to know the property but them better as well. One could not ask for more interested, involved, and encouraging clients than Elsie Thompson and Sandy Wilson have been. By the end of the process, one feels like a member of the family.

In addition to thanking Elsie and Sandy for their wholehearted support, I am deeply indebted to Calder Loth and Dr. Dan Vivian for their contributions. I met Mr. Loth at a Stratford Hall Cultural Landscape Symposium several years ago and it was immediately apparent that if there was anything to know about historic architecture in Virginia, he knew it. He graciously reviewed the manuscript, provided helpful comments and illustrations, and has provided his recollections of The Tuleyries for inclusion in the book. My friend and former professor, Dan Vivian, has for the third time reviewed one of my manuscripts and for the second has provided an introduction for one of them. The world would be a much better place if all professors were so unstintingly supportive of their former students.

Thanks are due to many others who assisted along the way, including the staff of the Clarke County Historical Association and to John Milner and Christina Henry Carter for taking the time to discuss the restoration process in detail. I am also grateful to those helped with images: Ginny Dunn, The Library of Virginia; Matthew Guillen, Virginia Museum of History & Culture; Robert Hancock, White House of the Confederacy - The American Civil War Museum; Nancy Comer, Handley Regional Library; Loren Culver, R. W. Norton Museum; and Ocean's Bridge. Proving that it is always better to be lucky than good, I am thrilled to thank Mrs. F. W. McM. Woodrow for the image of Mary Tuley's beautiful portrait. I could not now for the life of me reconstruct how I managed to find her but her kindness in providing the image not only proved an unexpected birthday present but added greatly to the visual understanding of the Tuleys and their world.

A further word about images is in order. Those not otherwise credited are either from the Wilson family archives or were taken by me. Concerning quotations of text, they have been presented as written, to the best of my ability to read them. Any errors in that process or otherwise are my own.

Finally, I hope that my efforts will serve as a pleasant reminder to the Wilson family of their time at The Tuleyries, will give pleasure and perspective to its new owners, and be enjoyed by all those who appreciate historic architecture and fascinating history.

John David Myles, October 5, 2020

REFERENCES

A Complete Body of Architecture, Isaac Ware, T. Osborn and J. Shipton (London 1756)

An Illustrated Glossary of Early Southern Architecture & Landscape, Carl R. Lounsbury, Oxford University Press (New York 1994)

americanrails.com/gould.html

Annals of Clarke County Virginia, Volume I, Stuart E. Brown Jr. ed., Virginia Book Company (Berryville 1983)

Annals of Clarke County Virginia, Volume IV, Lorraine F. Myers and Stuart E. Brown Jr. eds., Virginia Book Company (Berryville 2002)

Architecture of the Old South - Virginia, Mills Lane, Beehive Press (Savannah 1987)

Archives and papers at The Tuleyries

A Separate Place, Warren R. Hofstra, Clarke County Sesquicentennial Committee (White Post 1986)

Benito Quinquela Martin From the Docks of La Boca to the Walls of St James's Palace: The Extraordinary Success of a Foundling Turned Coal Worker Turned Artist, Anne Claiborne Thompson, unpublished master's thesis for the University of Edinburgh (2011)

Baltimore Directory, Richard T. Matchett (Baltimore 1833)

Birth of a Virginia Plantation House, Peter Hodson, Calder Loth, ed., Center for Palladian Studies in America, Inc. (Richmond 2012)

civilwarintheeast.com/things/timeline-shenandoah-61-62/, Steve A. Hawks (2019)

civilwarintheeast.com/things/timeline-shenandoah-64/, Steve A. Hawks (2020)

Clarke County (Images of America), Maral S. Kalbian, Arcadia Publishing (Charleston, South Carolina 2011)

Court Circles of the Republic, Mrs. E. F. Ellet, Philadelphia Publishing Company (Philadelphia 1869)

encyclopediavirginia.org/Mahone_William_1826-1895, Peter C. Luebke (2016)

encyclopediavirginia.org/Shenandoah_Valley_during_the_Civil_War, Paul Christopher Anderson (2015)

Historic Homes of Northern Virginia, John W. Wayland, The McClure Company (Staunton 1937)

Historical Register and Dictionary of the United States Army, From its Organization, September 29, 1789 to March 2, 1903, Francis B. Hertman, Government Printing Office (Washington 1903)

History of Clarke County, Virginia, Thos. D. Gold and C. R. Hughes (Berryville 1914)

history.state.gov/departmenthistory/people

In the Shadow of the Blue Ridge, Mary Gray Farland and Beverley Bigelow Byrd, William Byrd Press (Richmond 1979)

Iron Horses in the Valley: The Valley and Shenandoah Valley Railroads, 1866-1882, John R. Hildebrand, Burd Street Press (Shippensburg, Pennsylvania 2001)

National Register of Historic Places Inventory - Nomination Form, The Tuleyries, 72001388, August 7, 1972

National Register of Historic Places Inventory - Nomination Form, Millwood Colored School, 00001431, November 22, 2000

Norfolk & Western's Shenandoah Valley Line, Mason Y. Cooper, The Norfolk & Western Historical Society (Roanoke 1998)

nps.gov/cebe/learn/historyculture/the-burning.htm

philadelphiabuildings.org/pab/app/ar_display.cfm/26050, Sandra Tratman

Preservation and Restoration Survey for The Tuleyries, John Milner Associates for Mr. and Mrs. Orme Wilson Jr. (West Chester, Pennsylvania 1989)

Records of the Clarke County Circuit Clerk

Records of the Clarke County Recorder

rct.uk/collection/search#/1/collection/405246/george-ii-1683-1760

Some Important Virginia Specimens in the National Institution for the Promotion of Science, David W. Johnston, *Banisteria*, Virginia Natural History Society (Martinsville Number 10, 1997)

St. Paul's The Cathedral Church of London 604-2004, Derek Keene, Arthur Burns, and Andrew Saint, eds., Yale University Press (New Haven and London 2004)

The Blandy Experimental Farm, A History, Thelma L. Schmidhauser, unpublished manuscript, 1986

The Field Illustrated, The Return of the Hereford, Robert V. Hoffman (New York Vol. XXVI-No. 8, August, 1916)

The Papers of Jefferson Davis, Volume 3, July 1846-December 1848, James T. McIntosh, ed., Louisiana State University Press (Baton Rouge 1981)

The Tuley Family Memoirs, William Floyd Tuley, W. T. Hedden Printer (New Albany, Indiana 1906)

These Truths, Jill Lepore, W. W. Norton & Company (New York 2018)

Tuleyries Farm, R. E. Griffith Sr., unpublished manuscript (Winchester 1936)

Uncommon Vernacular, John C. Allen, Jr., West Virginia University Press (Morgantown 2011)

U. S. Army Center of Military History, history.army.mil.books

Virginia Patents, A. J. Morrison, William and Mary College Quarterly Historical Magazine (Williamsburg Vol. II, No. 3, July 1922)

Young Carpenter's Guide, Owen Biddle, Johnson & Warner (Richmond 1815)

INDEX